The ABCs of Caregiving

Part 2

Essential Information for You and Your Family

Nanette J. Davis, Ph.D.

A House of Harmony Press Publication

The ABCs of Caregiving, Part 2
Essential Information for You and Your Family

©2015 Nanette J. Davis, Ph.D.

A House of Harmony Press Publication
Bellingham, WA
www.houseofharmonypress.com

This book is not intended as a substitute for the medical advice of qualified health care professionals. The reader should regularly consult a physician in matters relating to personal health for themselves or their care receivers, and particularly with respect to any symptoms that may require diagnosis or medical attention.

print ISBN: 978-0-9838299-7-3
e-book ISBN: 978-0-9838299-6-6

Publisher's Cataloging-in-Publication Data pending

Book design and typesetting for print and ebook:
Kate Weisel, www.weiselcreative.com

Cover photo: ©Merkushev | Dreamstime.com

To those whose love, care
and kindness make life
better for others.

Contents

L

M

N

O

P

Q

R

Foreword

When I began my research on caregiving in 2005, I had no idea it would be transformed into 60 interviews, four books and numerous articles and posts. Writing about caregiving allowed me to accomplish three long-cherished goals: 1) Interview women who may have shared my own intense experience in caring for a loved one; 2) clarify the profound importance of family caregiving as a sacrificial act; and 3) provide a foundation for personal growth for caregivers, which includes *awareness*, *education* and *enlightenment* about the nature of giving care.

My first book on caregiving, *Blessed is She,* presented the initial set of caregiver narratives, focusing on the trials, tribulations and triumphs of women confronted with long-term care of elderly relatives or friends. *Caregiving Our Loved Ones,* the second book, was *a re-envisioning* of the caregiver narratives, and included more of my own personal experiences as a long-term caregiver for my husband. I also developed a "Lessons Learned" section for each chapter, paying more attention to ways caregivers can surmount the caregiving burden.

My readers then urged me to write a simpler, inspirational book that could enhance the caregiver's spiritual life. This resulted in *The ABCs of Caregiving: Words to Inspire You.* And, finally, a companion book, this undertaking: *The ABCs of Caregiving, Part 2: Essential Information for You and Your Family*, offering practical guidelines for steering the caregiver's ship through the often stormy seas of long-term care.

In all honesty, I admit that my own caregiving duties over time seemed to become increasingly heavy. As my late husband's illness became more debilitating, I found myself less sure, even to the point of feeling helpless and out of control. Watching him decline, I feared for my own physical and mental health. Realizing I couldn't do it alone, I began taking steps. First, I created a family care team. Next, I went to a counselor each week. Then, I sought caregiving assistance in the home. Later, I moved my husband into care. Despite my deep reluctance, I recognized that our family's Herculean, but inadequate, efforts to keep him at home were simply not working.

We often presume that the caregiver operates as a lone wolf, a brilliant beacon on the uncertain shoals of elder care. Confident that they are doing the right thing for their loved one, they forge their way in and out of doctors' offices, hospitals, care centers and adult day health facilities. But the caregivers I interviewed—and the dozens of caregivers I have spoken to since that time—did not have that sense of certainty about their decisions.

Initially, many of these caregivers had only a limited grasp of their loved one's medical condition, treatment, outcome, support structures and the boundless demands they would confront along the caregiving path. Only when they woke up to the reality that they had to devise a caregiving strategy that specifically worked for *them* and their *family* that included these three basics—*awareness, education* and, eventually, *enlightenment*—could they move with self-assurance, knowing they had taken the best course of action possible.

This approach to caregiving leaves out the "shoulds," "musts," "have-to's" and any actions that do not add up to a recipe for successful caregiving. Once you can move beyond the reluctant or insecure caregiver stage, you may find that caregiving can be the journey of a lifetime. And like all sojourns, events arrive unannounced—the good, bad and indifferent. Your task will be to do the best you can to prepare for any and all contingencies.

Getting into the flow of care, you may discover caregiving is what you make it. It may provide an opportunity to set things right, clear out the cobwebs from a relationship, jettison those fractured feelings, and perhaps, rectify the past. Or caregiving can be a renewal, allowing you a rare glimpse of your loved one's inner self, as they struggle with terminal illness and dying. Best of all, you can transform caregiving into the most mindful experience of your life.

This book offers a first step toward shaping your caregiving perspective: information that puts you in the driver's seat. Managing caregiving actually does have some general requirements: get the correct information *when* you need it, ask for help *before* you are overwhelmed, seek the *best* advice, and never turn down *support* from any reliable source.

And, similar to any management job, it can be most effectively handled with goal setting, staying level-headed and rewarding supporters. Goals can be simple or complex: giving your loved one a backrub today or checking out local care facilities to prepare for the time when he or she may be ready. Keeping your own health and emotions intact may take more time and effort, but it is well worth it. You'll have renewed energy for assisting your loved one.

Rewarding your supporters may sound far-fetched, but you might be surprised how effective you can be with an appreciative note to a ward nurse for a job well done, a thankful phone call to an obliging neighbor or a gift certificate to a friend who held your hand during an especially rocky time. You may find they'll be back to give more aid and assistance when you need it most. My experiences taught me that one needs only a simple prescription to be a compassionate caregiver: Unlock your mind and open your heart, and let the light stream through you.

Not everyone has had the good fortune to bring their work, week after week, to a scintillating writers' group. I thank you one and all—Evelyn Wright, Lynne Masland, Iris Jones, Amelia Pryor and Troy Faith Ward—for your trenchant insights, comments and criticisms that have kept me on target. Once again, Susan Browne and Patricia Davis—my unerring, editor-in-chief daughters—have cleared up the patchy sentences and allowed the prose an open road.

I owe a particular debt of gratitude to two other readers of my manuscript. Kate Massey, Family Caregiver Support Specialist at the Northwest Regional Council, brought new insights to nearly every page. Claudia Rumwell, who created a must-have for every caregiver, *The Senior Care Organizer* (www.seniorcareorganizer. com), provided many a useful suggestion.

For Burl, loving husband, dear friend and ever-faithful grammarian and cheering section, I could never have done without your constant encouragement.

A personal aside:

> *Nanette to Burl – I hope you can forgive those late dinners and missed appointments, while I was hammering away on the keyboard.*

> *Burl to Nanette – To have been in the "catbird seat" and have witnessed a life so well-lived in the face of family catastrophe, I could not entertain any apology or need for forgiveness.*

⚮⚭ *A* ⚬⚭

*A*ctivity – Let's explore some simple exercises for caregivers to get active. In just 10-minute units, you can get out of that afternoon slump and start feeling better. Of course, check with your doctor to see what level and intensity of exercise is most appropriate for you. And don't forget to cool down, and have a large glass of water after any physical exertion.

Here's how it's done. Health experts say we need to get 150 minutes or two-and-a-half hours of moderately intense exercise every week. That amounts to about 20 minutes a day. Why not try out some of the following, as recommended by the *Harvard Women's Health Watch*? Or be creative, and line up your own favorite brief calorie burners. Keep in mind that some exercises require longer periods of time to gain the benefits.

1. **Plant a garden** (*Calories burned in 10 minutes: 40-55*). Digging, hoeing, weeding and carrying tools from house to garden really do burn calories. Also, consider this. It not only works the muscles and lifts the spirits, but a garden of fresh

vegetables can provide the added benefit of promoting a healthy diet.

2. **Walk the dog** (*Calories burned in 10 minutes: 40-50*). Dogs make great exercise buddies, and dog owners are far more likely to meet the government's physical activity recommendation than those who don't have a dog. To gain maximum benefit, let your pet finish his "business," before you start your exercise clock. And don't forget: keep up a brisk pace to get the most out of dog walking.

3. **Clean house** (*Calories burned in 10 minutes: 45-50*). Housework may not be your idea of exercise, but you'd be surprised how using old-fashioned elbow grease can help you get fitter. Put aside the mechanical aids and go for the broom and mop. When washing the dishes, you can stand on one leg—then the other—to improve your balance. When you breathe deeply along with the exercise, you gain the additional benefit of relaxation.

4. **Play with the children or grandchildren** (*Calories burned in 10 minutes: 40-60*). Instead of passively reading a story or sitting on a park bench, try playing right along with the kids. Hide-and-seek, playing ball, pushing them on a swing and bustling around the park can be a bright spot in everyone's day and get your heart rate going.

5. **Walk the neighborhood** (*Calories burned in 10*

minutes: 40-50). Nothing suits a busy caregiver better than moving outside for fresh air and sunshine. I guarantee it. You'll feel rejuvenated and reinvigorated. You might want to plug in some music to give you an extra boost as you circle around your familiar territory.

6. **Practice Yoga** (*Calories burned depend on the person and type of yoga. Count on at least 100-plus per hour*). When you talk with your friend about her yoga workout, she'll rarely discuss weight loss or calorie burn. People flock to yoga for its mind/body connection, the sense of oneness and ease you feel. It teaches us to listen to our bodies and naturally avoid unhealthy behaviors. That should be recommendation enough.

Yoga need not be your sole means of exercise, though. If you have the time and motivation, try cycling, running or vigorous dancing. These burn a lot more calories per hour compared to yoga.

7. **Swimming** (*Calories for one hour of laps,* 476). If you can find a longer stretch of time during your day, you'll discover swimming in your local pool to be an ideal exercise. It's easy on the joints, strengthens your lungs and serves as a full-body, aerobic workout. What's more, swimming is calming, counters daily stress and is especially refreshing during the warmer months of the year.

No matter your age, exercise helps keep your weight down and maintain good cardiovascular health. Other reasons why you should get off the couch and try regular exercise include: (1) better overall health, (2) improved mood and (3) stronger bones. For older adults in particular, regular exercise reduces the risk of cognitive impairment and falling.

If you can't get out of the house or spend time away from your loved one, an exercise bike or mini stepper could be a lifesaver.

Start with those first steps: Get yourself in gear, and then stick with it!

*A*dvocacy: **Doctor's Visit** – Being an effective health care advocate for your loved one is the quickest way to empower you as a caregiver. Rarely an easy task, advocating for your relative can get downright complicated when attempting to navigate the maze of options. Here are a handful of indispensable tips to help you through the process of dealing with medical staff and routines.

Let's start with doctors' visits, which can be fraught with tension. Typically, you may be shunted from specialist to specialist during the diagnostic phase. In fact, caregivers often find themselves pulled into a revolving door of medical practitioners. Many of these physicians may seem impersonal and uninvolved with your case. Get ready for three stages of advocacy for each medical encounter: before the doctor's visit, during the doctor's visit, and after the doctor's visit.

Planning is foremost. Obtain an Advanced Health

Care Directive, which tells your family, friends and medical providers your loved one's health care preferences for diagnostic testing, procedures, resuscitation and organ donation. Keep a log or journal with changes in behavior, pain levels, new symptoms, and most important, questions you want the doctor to answer. Give yourself and your loved one plenty of time to get ready with a minimum of stress.

Finally, your visits will go much smoother if you have something to occupy your loved one during the inevitable wait, perhaps a game or a picture book.

During the doctor's visit, it's useful to be upfront with the doctor, who typically talks to the caregiver, rather than the patient. Be certain the doctor talks directly to your loved one in simple English. Inquiring about Medicare, insurance, out-of-pocket costs and medications will be at the top of your list. You will want to identify when your loved one is experiencing an emergency medical situation, and what to do about it. Ask your doctor for specific information about home health care or Hospice when needed. You may wish to take notes during the meeting so you can review all the information. It can be overwhelming to remember it all.

Following up on the doctor's visit can be equally important for good health care for your loved one. If you're uncomfortable with the doctor's information or prescriptions, you may wish to have a second opinion or check with your insurance company. With an Advanced Health Care Directive, you have a right to the medical records of your loved one. Ask for records after a hospital stay or from a specialist to ensure your primary physician stays up-to-date. Although your emotional energy will be limited, don't put up with the medical expert who says, "Just trust me." You need to be the final decision-maker along with your loved one, if capable.

As for medical prescriptions, using the same pharmacy is strongly recommended to avoid drug interaction effects and overprescribing. You'll find pharmacists are very helpful in explaining some of the more common side effects of any particular medication.

If you intend to use a home care agency for in-home nursing help, be sure the person is insured, bonded and has worker's compensation. It's also a good idea to carefully interview the person who will be assisting your loved one to get the best fit for your needs. Prior planning takes the guesswork out of your health care interactions. If you're organized and have done your homework, everyone benefits.

*A*dvocacy: Hospital or Emergency Room – Advocacy is at its most crucial when a crisis occurs and your loved one has an emergency. Communication is key, beginning with the reason for bringing in your loved one. Be very clear if you believe they are having a heart attack or stroke. Keep a copy of your loved one's medications, dosages and usages, as well as all of his or her medical conditions. A special proviso when your loved one can't communicate is to carry the Advanced Healthcare Directive at all times. Or provide the information to the hospital even before an emergency occurs. Because of long waits in emergency rooms, it's advisable to keep a bag of supplies in the trunk of your car. Water, snacks, a book, and your own medicine will get you through those interminable delays.

Hospital food can be less than appetizing. Worse, it can be downright unhealthy, especially for diabetics, obese persons or those with food allergies. Contact the hospital dietician at the outset to ensure the food served is right for your patient. You may also need to monitor your loved one's medications. Should they be taken *with* or *without* food? How about the time of day? Some illnesses require very specific instructions from the pharmacist. Read the labels and check with your doctor or pharmacist to make certain medications are dispensed correctly. These recommendations also apply to stays in rehabilitation or long-term care facilities.

*A*dvocacy: **Skilled Nursing Facility** – This arena may be the most challenging because you simply cannot look out for your loved one 24/7. You *can* take a few steps to alleviate the hardships your loved one is likely to confront. Let's start with the basics. Care center residents have the same needs as anyone else—namely, a desire for recognition as an individual—in this case, one who has special needs because of physical and mental infirmities.

Without individual recognition, residents can feel displaced and, without a sense of familiarity, feel virtually homeless. Depression and withdrawal soon follow. Your concerned presence will be crucial for smoothing over the rough patches. Engaging the staff with your loved one remains the best remedy for dislocation in an institutional setting. When you develop a relationship with nursing facility staff, it makes the rest of the advocacy job much simpler. Rather than asking the patient to change life-long individual habits, insist that the facility make adjustments in routines.

Individualized care is the basic tenet of the standards set forth by the federally sponsored Nursing Home Reform Law, and it applies to all skilled nursing facilities receiving federal money. Staff can provide individualized care by carefully assessing each resident, and then developing a plan of care to meet that person's needs. The plan must then be publicized throughout the institution (i.e., kitchen staff, physical therapists, nursing staff) to ensure its implementation.

To enhance individualized care, try setting up a memory box outside the loved one's bedroom door. Within the frame, you can include photos, letters and other small momentos. With all rooms looking alike, the memory box helps the resident locate his or her bedroom, as well as serves to recall cherished memories. Staff respond positively to memorabilia displays as they see room occupants become transformed into real flesh and blood persons with rich and compelling lives.

You can solicit your family to play a significant role in advocacy, as well. Family members can help you by making regular visits, sharing information with the nursing staff, participating in care meetings and expecting the facility to make reasonable accommodations for your relative's individual needs and preferences.

Be on the lookout for inadequate staffing or absence of staff during busy times, such as bedtime and early morning. Rehabilitation centers are required by law to maintain certain levels of care. You will find an ombudsman available in your area or state, who will listen and act upon staffing or other complaints you may have. (See also Ombudsman.)

You will want to review the care center's assessment of your loved one's medical condition. The assessment serves as the basis for understanding the person's ability to walk, talk, remember, bathe, see, hear, eat, dress and comprehend. The evaluation also determines the level of assistance required for toileting, wheelchair transfers, physical therapy and other needs. A solid assessment considers personal habits and preferences, such as the best time for waking up in the morning or favorite television shows. Familiar routines, activities, habits and relationships are precious reminders of our individuality. Skilled nursing facilities employing the one-size-fits-all model frequently ignore the "specialness" of each person in their care, which results in inadvertently undermining the resident's sense of self. It will be your job to see that your expectations are being met.

A final note. Frequent visits at different times of the day while your loved one is in care can reveal essential information about the treatment. Use a checklist for questions and concerns, and bring them to the administrator's attention. Regular, even daily, visits also lift your loved one's spirits as he or she copes with an unfamiliar environment. Bringing photos and other memorabilia from home also fosters your loved one's acceptance, especially if the person must remain in the facility. As a caregiving friend recently said: "If you have a team of advocates, your loved one will be all right."

*A*ging in Place /Aging in Community – When we hear the term, *aging in place*, we think of keeping our loved one in the comfort, convenience and safety of their own home, as opposed to a health care facility. What exactly does this encompass?

Aging in place implies that an older person, ideally with adequate assistance from a caregiver, can help maintain a full range of normal daily activities, including transportation, shopping, cooking, cleaning, home and garden maintenance, and a host of ordinary tasks that are taken for granted among younger, healthy people. And a living situation that works at 70 years of age—when independence is less likely to be an issue—may not be the case for a frail 90-year-old still residing in the family home. Along with the older person's caregiver, family, friends and neighbors can pitch in from time to time, but the optimal scenario requires a community effort to make aging in place a reality over the long term.

Aging in Community offers a more broad-based approach than the limited notion of staying in the family home or down-sized condo. Baby Boomers have watched their overtaxed parents struggle with aging by themselves, often isolated and lonely. Now these mid-lifers are seeking a more expansive model for their own aging, which embraces the idea of being "in community."

The newer model has two primary elements: staying active and involved as long as possible in their chosen home and reimagining existing care facilities. This could easily incorporate living in a long-term care facility—assisted living or skilled nursing—but without the trappings of an institutional setting, which are habitually overcrowded, understaffed, impersonal, and monotonous.

Eden Alternative

Dr. Bill Thomas was primarily concerned with emotional well-being when he conceived of the *Eden Alternative* in the early 1990s as a way to alleviate the loneliness, helplessness and boredom that permeated the nursing home he operated in New York. "What good is quality of medical care if your life is miserable?" he asked.

Thomas' original vision of the Eden Alternative focused on partnering with nursing homes to help them change their culture and environment to "create a habitat for human beings rather than facilities for the frail and elderly." An Eden-certified nursing home moves away from the sterility of the long-term care environment toward creating a setting where personal care dominates and cohesive principles enliven both residents and staff.

Eden homes aim to 1) create a home-like atmosphere; 2) make a difference in elderly people's lives; 3) change the culture of care; 4) train and support staff; and 5) love, care, and live together as a family. The Eden principles have been incorporated in pre-existing long-term facilities, where a menagerie of dogs, cats, birds and children (who may be part of an in-house daycare program) create appealing and warm living spaces.

Happily, measurable medical benefits followed Thomas' inventive approach. After two years, his first Eden facility had 50 percent fewer infections and 25 percent fewer deaths than a comparable non-Eden nursing home. Other studies show that even bedsores and dementia can be significantly reduced using the Eden Alternative.

Green House Project

Moving away from institutional settings, Thomas went on to develop another innovative method: The "Green House Project." Now, more than 100 homes have been built, starting with the idea of helping companies and individuals convert or build residential homes. The Project's primary goal is to provide high levels of care for persons who do not wish to be in a nursing home setting. Among other supporters, the Robert Wood Johnson Foundation has funded an innovative design, involving clusters of smaller "green" homes, built for six to ten senior residents, with outdoor space and gardens. Each resident has a private bath and bedroom, and has access to shared areas of the house at any time, enhancing sociability and autonomy, streamlining delivery of services and creating a homey environment.

The Village

Two additional models have emerged as workable for those open to aging in community: the Village and Care Circles. The Village is designed for people who want to develop the kinds of supports for their old age that families used to provide (some still do), but which are increasingly rare for a variety of reasons. Villages are sustained by members or their caregivers, who contribute financially, with costs depending on how extensive the level of services and number of members. For example, overall costs for members of a "typical" Village run about $80,000 for start-up expenditures and $20,000 to $200,000 to maintain it each year.

A group of Boston seniors in the Beacon Hill District initiated the first Village in 2001 to help one another live as long as possible in their neighborhood. Now the Beacon Hill Village is an independent, non-profit organization, governed by the members themselves and supported by members' dues and external donations and grants. A host of "partners," including preferred providers, member volunteers and community services help its members to age in place and connect with their broader community.

Over a 13-year period, 140 established Villages have emerged with more than 200 on the way, with budgets ranging from $1,000 to $674,000, depending on the size of the membership.

Villages promise a higher quality of life by coordinating paid and volunteer elder services with a single phone call. The more developed Village provides a dense network of volunteer, agency and professional intervention that can sustain an older person and their caregivers over time. Services range from education on aging/caregiving issues and elder law to geriatric care and money management. Preferred providers are vetted by the Village, who oversee the quality of services, and paid professionals are encouraged to offer discounts to members.

Volunteers play a significant role in this project, as younger and healthy people "pay it forward" to bring various services to disabled seniors, helping them with chores, meals, home maintenance and other services. In turn, volunteers receive benefits or assistance in the future, especially gratifying for older volunteers. All Villages depend heavily upon trained volunteers, which can substantially reduce costs for members.

Care Circles

Another highly successful model for aging in place, the Care Circle, offers a more nurturing approach, operating on the principle of "a step forward in giving back." Initially, care circles were developed by the Australian government in the 1990s to reduce the Aborigine people's social problems. Transplanted to North America, care circles have become a substitute for the extended family or small community for better addressing the needs of disabled and elderly persons.

Care circles are privately organized social networks of friends, family, neighbors and volunteers that help seniors experience round-the-clock attention through individualized care plans. Care circles work on the premise that shared lives and real relationships define the central values of aging in community. These networks stress interdependence, not merely independence, among those in need.

Multifaceted by design, care circles move beyond the delivery of services into a full-fledged model of care, support and shared lives, ultimately helping elders to maintain the life they desire in community with others.

A few highlights of the care circle:

1. Operates in any neighborhood, larger community or care facility.

2. Embraces all age and income groups.

3. Aims to lessen the caregiver burden by offering hands-on assistance to caregivers working with ill and disabled seniors *without cost* (unless seeking professional or business assistance).

4. Addresses head-on the incredibly difficult role of middle-aged caregivers, the "sandwich generation," who are squeezed between the stresses of caring for both parents and children.

5. Recognizes the priorities established by the World Health Organization to influence the health and quality of life of older people, including transportation, social participation and connectivity.

To create your own care circle program, you can seek technical assistance from an organization, such as Lotsa Helping Hands, that will schedule medications, transportation, meal planning, and the like to fit the needs and lifestyle of the elderly person. Volunteers sign up through the website, and choose a specific assignment for assisting a needy person.

Numbers tell the story. Members of Lotsa Helping Hands have offered mutual help and care for seniors and their caregivers to more than 1.3 million members and 70,000 communities, successfully delivering 1,400,000 meals and a multitude of other services since its inception. Volunteers sign up to help only one person at a time on a regimented, yet flexible, schedule. This ensures that no one volunteer will be saddled with excessive duties nor will the elderly person or their caregiver be swamped with surplus attendants.

The one constant throughout the process of aging is change. Local care circle members' roles and responsibilities will undoubtedly undergo transformation as a result of elderly persons' changes in vision, hearing, physical stamina, sleep habits and nutritional needs.

Private companies that charge for setting up services, such as "CareCircle SAP" care programs, have now entered the arena. The company works with both patient and family/friends to develop a care plan that will accommodate a variety of patient needs: visits, meals, housekeeping, transportation and chores, as well as assist with drug delivery or schedule medical and social services. The company offers a free app through iTunes that helps patients and their families find the best care practices from experts and caregivers around the world.

Aside from assembling health and welfare collaborators and expanding the circle of mutual support, both

Villages and care circles offer a host of "little things" that people can do for each other. The goal is to make it easier for older people to stay in their home or care facility, and enjoy their time with family and friends. For many seniors, it can be an empowering experience.

Caregivers can gain a measure of freedom when they know it's possible for their loved one to get a ride to the doctor, receive a hot meal or have a regular visitor. Volunteers can also help seniors make a home or life in a facility more comfortable and user friendly as the senior ages. It's remarkable how relieved caregivers can be with a volunteer checking in on their loved one from time to time, especially if the caregiver is working or the senior is living alone. Without doubt, these innovative programs—Eden Alternative, Green House Project, Villages and care circles—address the many issues of aging in place in our diverse communities across America.

Assisted Living – A generation ago, when an older or disabled person needed extra help, they had no choice but to move to a long-term care facility, even if they didn't need the extensive nursing services. Today, assisted living is a marketing term that refers to a type of living arrangement in which personal care services are available that run the gamut from housekeeping to minor medical assistance.

Although each state has its own licensing requirements, many states are seeking to unify assisted living provisions and to develop a common model for all states. For instance, names for this form of congregate living vary widely: assisted living, residential care, personal care, board and care, adult family home, adult foster care, adult group home, community-based support care, and so forth.

Regardless of terminology, *assisted living* fills the gap between home care and skilled nursing facility. As a fairly new alternative, assisted living provides a more home-like environment for people needing or anticipating help with activities, but don't need the round-the-clock medical care and supervision of a care center. It differs from a *retirement facility*, in that residents of assisted living are no longer able to lead independent lives, but are dependent on staff for a variety of everyday needs.

Here is a list of typical services found in assisted living facilities:

- Three meals a day served in a common dining area.
- Assistance with eating.
- Assistance with bathing, dressing, toileting, and walking.
- Housekeeping services.
- Transportation.
- Emergency call systems in each resident's living space.
- Exercise and wellness programs.
- Medication management.
- Laundry services.
- Social and recreational activities.

- Staff available to help with scheduled needs, as well as unexpected issues.
- Access to health and medical services.
- 24-hour security.

Assisted living facilities are owned and operated by both for-profit and non-profit organizations, and can range widely in costs. A resident can generally expect to pay between $2,000 to $5,000 every month (compared with $5,000 to $10,000 and up for a long-term nursing facility). How can most families pay for these high costs of care? Here are some creative ways to afford assisted living. In many cases, it's advisable to use more than one source of income.

1. **Pay for assisted living with veterans' benefits.** The Veteran's Administration (VA) offers Aid and Attendance as part of the "Improved Pension" Benefit, which is available to any veteran or surviving spouse who is disabled and whose income is below a certain limit. Applying for veterans' benefits can be a time-consuming and frustrating experience. Typically, the facility offers the services of a benefits administrator, who works with the family to help obtain the maximum benefits for which the person qualifies. Be prepared for long waits with the Veteran's Administration, though.

2. **Pay for assisted living with Social Security payments.** Although Social Security monthly income is rarely enough to cover all the expenses of

assisted living, it can be a solid "down payment" along with other funding sources. Your local, state or federal Area Agency on Aging can advise you about a free consultation from a *Government Health Insurance Counselor* to help navigate through the maze of bureaucratic requirements for any public benefits available to you. Do not count on Medicaid or Medicare, federal health insurance programs, to cover assisted living expenses. These programs are primarily geared to pay for hospital care and rehabilitation in skilled nursing facilities.

3. **Pay for assisted living with a life insurance policy.** Life insurance does more than pay out after the death of a beneficiary. It can provide financial support now, when the money is most needed. To cash out your policy, ask your life insurance company about "accelerated" or "living" benefits. Usually the company that originally issued the policy buys it back for 50 to 75 percent of its face value. Different rules may apply depending on the company and type of policy. If the life insurance company refuses to give you cash benefits, you can look into a life settlement company that buys policies in return for a "life settlement" or "senior settlement," which is usually a lump sum of 50 to 75 percent of the policy's face value. After buying the policy, the settlement company pays the premiums until the policyholder dies, at which point, the settlement company receives the

remainder of the policy value (not the original beneficiary). Check with your insurance agent for details on cashing out a policy.

4. **Pay for assisted living with long-term care insurance.** If your loved one has a long-term care insurance policy that pays for assisted living, they may be in luck. Be certain to read the small print to determine what mental or physical diagnosis covers a person in the facility. Policies usually have a designated payment, which can be paid to the beneficiary, which can then be turned over to the assisted living facility. Again, this is a standard form of insurance, so work with your insurance agent on this program.

5. **Pay for assisted living with an annuity.** An annuity may be a good option because the beneficiary has already paid a lump sum up front and has received or will be receiving regular payments back over a promised period of time. A warning: annuities are complex financial tools. Caregivers may wish to consult a trusted financial advisor about what annuity options would be most appropriate. Unfortunately, *annuity fraud* is more common than most of us realize. Be wary of the "too good to be true" financial plan—it undoubtedly is just that. Advice to the wary on investing in annuities: investigate, investigate, investigate.

6. **Pay for assisted living with a reverse mortgage.** If your loved one owns their home outright, or

has only a small mortgage on it, a reverse mortgage allows a cash-out on the value of the home equity. This can be paid out in a lump sum, or a series of monthly payments. The bank determines the value of what the home is worth and interest rates, taking into consideration their age and other factors, with the loan balance gradually increasing in time.

Reverse mortgage payments can work in one of two ways. If a couple is involved, and one needs assisted living, and the other remains in the home, the monthly payouts of the reverse mortgage can take care of some of the costs of assisted living. Another alternative is for one or both elders to remain in the home, and pay for home health care for personal services, rather than receiving care outside the home. Either way, the borrower(s) can remain in the home until death, even if the loan balance exceeds the home's worth. Upon death, the loan balance must be repaid, which usually requires selling the home to pay off the bank. Fees are invariably involved with a reverse mortgage, so proceed with caution.

A reverse mortgage can be very advantageous for some seniors, but for others it could be a liability, especially if the senior wishes to leave the home for an inheritance. Again, consult with your financial advisor before making a decision on a reverse mortgage.

7. **Pay for assisted living by renting out the family home.** If only one parent is still living, or if both parents need assistance with daily living,

the family home can be an important resource. Selling the home to pay for assisted living is always an option, but for many families, selling the home while their parents are still alive is not a viable choice. Property management services can handle all the details of renting the property for a fixed fee until the house is ready to be sold.

Why Seniors May Prosper in Assisted Living

Only rarely will you find a senior who doesn't wholly resist—kicking and screaming—moving out of their home and into assisted living. Once they realize the considerable *benefits* of residential living, including a private apartment, many will come to call it "home sweet home."

Safety and *comfort* are significant features of all assisted living centers. Nearly all have security systems to prevent burglary or attack. Most assisted living apartments also have alert systems in the event of an emergency. And, simply having other people around makes communal living safer than being in a house alone.

Meals in assisted living may constitute the highlight of a senior's day where communal dining exposes them to company three times a day. Not everyone feels that sociable, though. So, apartments often come equipped with a refrigerator and microwave for snacks or those short-order repasts. The well-ordered facility will keep an eye on how well the elders eat to see if supplements or nutritional beverages (i.e., Ensure, Glucerna) are necessary.

Transportation may be the next biggest plus after dining for many seniors, who can no longer drive safely. Staff members drive seniors where they want to go, whether to doctors' visits, shopping, community events, even Sunday afternoon drives in the country, without the hassle of negotiating traffic and weather conditions.

Socialization is perhaps the single most important reason why many people, who initially insisted they hated assisted living, end up thriving. Many seniors staying in their home end up homebound, finding it increasingly difficult to drive or even walk around their own neighborhood, much less keep in contact with others. Significant lifelong friends may have health problems or have died. Loneliness remains a chronic concern among a large proportion of aging Americans.

Less worry would be on any senior's hit parade, and assisted living facilities accommodate this by handling all maintenance in their apartments, and keeping bill paying to an absolute minimum. Often, the phone bill is the only one that needs paying, aside from personal purchases. Home repairs, the muddle of sorting out contractors, bills mounting up —all are things of the past, leaving an abundance of time for enjoying life.

Activities may be what assisted living is all about. Unlike a nursing facility, with its primary emphasis on medication and nursing services, assisted living centers can fill a senior's day—and then some. Holidays of any kind become an excuse for crowding the calendar.

Highgate House, a local assisted living facility, where my late husband resided for over a year, offered an abundance of daily activities. Something for everyone, including, music and song, bingo, popcorn, various "happy hours," games, religious services, birthday parties, car outings, exercise, manicure parties for the ladies, movies, art therapy, news-of-the-day discussions, and more. And each day of the week had something different. I observed most seniors participated in a variety of events, but not to the point of taxing themselves.

The Downside of Assisted Living

On balance, assisted living fits some situations, but rarely all. Some seniors prefer to remain in their homes—disabilities and all. If accommodations for at-home living can be arranged, it might not be the best approach to force them out. Be prepared for sticker shock, however: Staying at home costs more than assisted living for round-the-clock attendants, who still need supervision by a responsible person.

Congregate living may prove difficult for certain persons who cannot adapt to communal style living. Additional hustle and bustle may be disconcerting for light sleepers or those who like to sleep late. Regimented mealtimes can discourage eaters who may not be hungry when the food is served. Elders are often finicky caters—some for health reasons—who resist eating certain foods, but are offered no choice. Some assisted living centers are chronically short of staff, and calls for help or apartment maintenance may be ignored or delayed.

Assisted living may be especially problematic when a person is seriously ill or dying, and eligible for end-of-life hospice care. A number of states—Idaho, Mississippi, Montana and North Dakota—won't allow hospice services to be provided on grounds that end-of-life residents are too demanding. Other states, including Alaska, Arkansas, Florida, Rhode Island, West Virginia and Vermont will allow *existing* residents to receive hospice services, but won't accept new residents who require end-of-life care.

Even with end-of-life care, a hospice nurse visits a patient only once or twice a week unless the person is in a crisis. Typically, for a hospice patient, a nurse's aide will come out several times weekly to help with bathing and other personal needs—hardly enough services for this demanding time. Family members will need to lend a hand or hire additional help if they choose to keep their loved one in assisted living.

Finally, tending to seriously ill persons with physician-prescribed "care kits" stocked with medications, such as morphine, Haldol and Ativan, to control pain may run counter to staff expectations and comfort levels. The hope of dying at home may not be fulfilled when the administration abruptly calls an ambulance to whisk the patient to the hospital to avoid emotionally disturbing their employees with an imminent death.

ℬ

*ℬ*ehavior Problems – When you are caring for a cognitively disabled person, you are quite likely to encounter profound, even difficult, and certainly *unpredictable,* behavior problems in your loved one. Few of us are prepared for the range of disturbing behavior that can compound the burden of care. Stories of demanding elderly parents, personality changes, hallucinations, temper tantrums, addictive behavior, even abuse, can terrify even the most experienced caregiver. Let's review some of the more typical problems, and offer some strategies for managing them.

Behavior Problem #1: Rage, Anger, Yelling

"Dad is really getting out of control with his constant anger and yelling."

Age and illness can intensify certain personality traits, often in unpleasant ways. An irritable person can become irascible, raging at anyone in sight, but especially the caregiver. The aging process itself can initiate distressful symptoms, as seniors vent their frustration about getting old, having chronic pain, losing friends, developing short-term memory issues, being incontinent, and other common difficulties. In some instances, intense and unprovoked anger can signal the onset of Alzheimer's disease or other neurological disorder.

Coping with anger could involve a number of strategies. Talk with your loved one about the underlying reason for the anger problem, whether medical, social or emotional, perhaps over coffee or in a comfortable setting. Focus on solutions. Talk about it over coffee. Set up an appointment with a professional. Be willing to consider medication. Take time out for yourself by finding a home health aide to fill in for you on a temporary or long-term basis. Put the spotlight on the positive. Get out in the fresh air. Call a friend. Do something you love. After diagnosing the source of the anger, and making certain that your loved one is cognitively able to understand you, lovingly confront your parent, spouse or relative and let them know that their outbursts are unacceptable. They must understand that you cannot continue to be their caregiver unless they curb their offensive behavior.

Behavior Problem #2: Abuse

"My sweet mother punched me the other day. What's happening to her?"

The same conditions that contribute to anger—chronic pain, losing friends, having memory issues, among others—can also generate abusive behavior in older adults. Stories of elderly parents who mentally, emotionally or physically abuse their caregivers are all too common. The causes for abuse range from personality disorders, substance abuse and mental illness to taking their frustrations out on those persons closest to them, even their son or daughter, because they feel safe to do so.

Managing this behavior may *require* professional help, whether it is a counselor or police. If the abuse is less drastic, speak out by telling your loved one how this behavior is harming both of you, as well as your relationship. Finding some respite for yourself may be essential for you to gain a much-needed perspective. *Never* accept unacceptable behavior. You have a right to your own life, free of abuse.

Behavior Problem #3: Neglecting Personal Hygiene and Self-Care

"My uncle just stopped shaving, putting on clean clothes, and absolutely refuses to take a shower."

Younger, healthy people can be quick to judge the older man or woman who wears dirty clothes, smells offensive, badly needs a shave or haircut, and otherwise appears unkempt. Caregivers feel especially frustrated when their loved one declines to take showers, wear fresh clothes and take care of personal hygiene. Caregivers may wonder: "Where does Uncle John's personal freedom end and my caregiver responsibility take over?"

Understanding *why* a loved one has let himself or herself go can be the key to finding a solution.

1. The issue may be *depression*. Seek professional

help. Counseling and medication could turn things around.

2. Another factor is *control.* As people age, they may lose more and more control over their lives. Death of friends, money worries, poor health, dementia or other conditions can undermine a person's sense of integrity. Be patient as you identify the reason for your loved one's worsening sense of well-being. Avoid nagging—they may resist more vigorously any efforts you make to change them. Consider lowering your standards and definition of cleanliness, as long as the person is not neglecting himself. Using humor and making a game out of the situation could win the day. "Say, Dad, remember when you said you always did look ridiculous with a shaggy beard? Betcha I can trim that in 5 minutes or less."

3. Sometimes a *decreased sense of sight and smell* may be at the root of the problem. A comment about "time for a shower and change" can bring them around. Or *memory* may be the issue. Days go by—who remembers Tuesday from Friday? It's so easy to lose track of time, and they don't realize how long it's been since they showered. Setting up a daily routine that you both agree on could be the answer.

4. *Fear or discomfort* can be a significant drawback to personal care. Fear of slipping in the tub, embarrassment about asking for help or physical

weakness can inhibit a frail or demented elder. A shower stool is one answer. Finding someone to help may be necessary, if the caregiver cannot manage alone. In any case, to ease the elder's fears, move gently and do not insist on a shower or bath. Perhaps try a sponge bath. Always ask permission before you begin, and then start by wiping the face and gradually moving to underarms and other parts of the body, telling them what you are doing as you go.

Behavior Problem #4: Swearing, Offensive Language and Inappropriate Comments

"Would you believe that Aunt Tess just used a litany of swear words when she told off poor Uncle Ben—and to think their 50th wedding anniversary is next Saturday."

Perhaps the most baffling behavior problem is when a normally loving parent or relative suddenly begins using profanities, speaking offensive language or saying insulting things. When the behavior is obviously out of character for a person, you are likely dealing with dementia. A number of suggestions might work here. Use distractions. Divert your elderly loved one's attention, which can be an effective technique to stop the swearing. Focus on evoking their long-term memory skills, allowing them to reminisce about their lives. You may find the elderly person has forgotten what set them off in the first place.

It's always advisable to pursue medical advice. In some instances, if nothing seems to be working, including medication and counseling, take a breath and wait for it to blow over.

Behavior Problem #5: Paranoia and Hallucinations

"Mom gets spooked every time the phone rings. She says, 'They're after me. I just know it's them.'"

Side effects of certain medications can contribute to a loved one seeing people who aren't there or believing someone is trying to harm them. Hallucinations and delusions in elders can also be a sign of physical illness, Alzheimer's disease or another neurological disorder. The deluded person may believe that what they are seeing, hearing or experiencing are real. First, investigate the concern. If they clearly are delusional, little can be achieved by trying to "talk them out of it."

Instead, first check with the doctor about changing prescriptions if you suspect medication to be the cause. Although each situation is different, I found some dementia patients think mirror images and shadows on the wall are actual people or the spirits of departed relatives. Lighting up dark corners and removing or covering up mirrors reduces these sources of concern. Certain hallucinations may, in fact, be comforting for a person. In such cases, going with the flow may be the best course of action.

Behavior Problem #6: Hoarding

"My mother won't throw out spoiled foods."

Unlike normal household clutter, hoarding behavior—acquiring and failing to throw out a large number of items—can be a major issue for caregivers. Hoarding could be an extension of a condition, such as deep-seated anxiety, which requires medication and therapy. Or, hoarding could reflect the onset of Alzheimer's, as the patient begins to collect and save out of fear of being overwhelmed by what lies ahead. Others hold on to items to preserve their memories, saving tangible reminders of the past.

A caregiver can intervene in a number of ways. Reasoning with the elder sometimes works, if you talk about items to throw out, give away or save. Creating a memory box could be a special place to keep beloved things. For food hoarders, I discovered that frequent cleaning of the fridge by either the caregiver or a family member is the easiest solution. Overflowing pantries and cupboards can go the way of other surplus items: out-the-door or stored. For "deep hoarders," caregivers may wish to consult an expert for other ways to deal with hoarding behavior, which may be masking mental illness, or may need to seek out someone that specializes in "dig outs."

Behavior Problem #7: Refusing to Let Outside Caregivers into Their Homes

"My parents' house is a mess, and the laundry is piling up."

As unlikely as it seems to inexperienced caregivers, many elderly or vulnerable persons reject any outsider, even well-meaning household help, from coming into their home. They may fear losing even more control. Or, it could reflect their weakness and inability to take care of their own needs. Before beginning any change, work to understand the extent of the elder's fear and distress. Take it slow: plan to have more than one serious talk about the issue. Once it sinks in that "we all need help from time to time," they may relent.

Start small, providing constant reassurance. One strategy may be to ask your loved one to "give it a try." Make it a one-month trial of having a housekeeper in for weekly vacuuming, taking out trash and washing clothes. Experienced senior care agencies also know how to handle situations like this, so consult them if necessary. Once your loved one becomes accustomed to having someone in the house, they may be fine with it.

Behavior Problem #8: Overspending or Extreme Frugality

"Help! My parents are at each other's throats. Dad won't spend a dime, and Mom has become a reckless shopaholic."

The ability to handle money is associated with independence, dependability and power. It's not unusual for age and disease to take away a person's capacity for managing their finances. Or, they begin compensating for other losses in their life, such as health problems or the death of friends. The inability to judge the financial picture accurately can lead to overestimating or underestimating actual funds. For over-spenders, when bad habits drain the budget leaving too little to pay the bills, or the older person requires others to step in and pay for expenses they should be able to manage, caregivers take heed.

Consider collecting receipts in an average month for

food, medicine and other basics, and showing them—in black and white—how much they need for living expenses. And then keep a close eye on the monthly budget. If the situation is more serious, the adult child may have to step aside and allow a third party to work with them. In a worse-case scenario, a money manager may have to be hired. You can check with the court for a protective order or consult an elder accountant or elder lawyer, who can provide you with names of reputable persons to handle their finances.

Hoarding money may be especially complicated for older persons. Frugality makes sense for those who lived through the Great Depression, World War II with rationing and extreme deprivation, past job losses, and countless other situations where money was virtually non-existent. For elders, it may feel natural to be fearful about "going broke" or "never having enough," especially after retirement and living on a reduced or fixed income.

Extreme frugality is another matter, however. When an elder refuses to pay for essential medicine, fresh food or heat for the house, it's time to take action. No one wants to see their loved one go without necessities. Caregivers can make other family members aware of changes that need to be made. If money is clearly available and the person is in denial, or refuses to spend it, even on essentials, this could be a serious mental health issue. Treating the anxiety that underlies the money hoarding is a good start. Medication and counseling can be a welcome remedy. Another strategy is helping the person sort out the monthly expenses and showing them there's plenty to go around.

Behavior Problem #9: Demanding All the Caregiver's Time and Attention

"I'm exhausted looking after Mom all the time, and not having a minute to care for my own family. She insists I spend every evening with her or she can't sleep."

We can understand how an older, sick person feels bereft and clings to the caregiver. An older parent or spouse may construe the caregiver's willingness as a round-the-clock commitment. When an overly demanding parent's claims threaten to overwhelm the caregiver's other priorities—work, family, recharging one's batteries—it is a recipe for caregiver burnout.

The key is to involve the isolated senior in community activities and adult day health, which provides social activities, meals, recreation and sometimes health-related services, as much as their capacities allow. Interaction with others combats the loneliness, and makes them somewhat less dependent on you. Another approach for the homebound elder is to consider a companion. Check with your parent's church or temple to see if they make social calls to shut-ins. Home health agencies and charitable organizations are other sources for trained companions. Don't expect that your elderly parent or spouse will be overjoyed with the new arrangement, at least at first. Time will soften the social distance you've had to create to maintain your own mental health during long-term caregiving.

C

*C*are Facilities – **When One Size Doesn't Fit All**
You've finally convinced your mom to move into a care facility near your home, only to discover that the facility isn't working out. After all that work of moving her from Stamford, Connecticut to Seattle—days of packing, organizing and letting go of family treasures—you and Mom have reluctantly agreed that this isn't the right place. You're both exhausted, and don't know what to do next.

Thousands of Americans find themselves in similar situations. You've placed your loved one in the "wrong" facility—great on the outside, but absolutely not a fit on the inside. Despite positive references from medical providers and even other caregivers, you can easily make the common mistake of assuming that one size fits all.

What to do? I recommend going back to the beginning. First, locate a facility that has respite or temporary care until you can locate the best possible place. Then, sit down and review all your loved one's needs—physical, mental, emotional and spiritual. Wound management? Wheelchair bound? Incontinent? Dementia?

Food disorder? Easily upset? Late riser? Religiously oriented? Depression? At the end of life? Identify as many markers as you can that will help you find just the right place for long-term care. Geriatric care managers or elder care advisors can be especially helpful for finding the right option.

Now, begin your grand tour of a few facilities you've selected that appear to fit your loved one's needs. You'll certainly want to interview a broad spectrum of staff at each facility: administrators, nurses, kitchen help, and anyone else who provides direct service to residents. Use your senses—sight, sound, smell, touch—and your intuition to detect the level, quality and quantity of care. Visit the facility at different times of the day. What kind of activities do they have? If it looks strictly custodial—just a place to park an older person—move on. That won't work for you. Try to tell the difference between staff efficiency and warmth; just getting the job done versus being committed to the residents.

Once you've made your decision, it's wise to stick around and follow up for a few weeks to ensure that the care plan is actually being carried out. Don't take "no" or "we're too busy right now" for an answer. Let administrators and staff know that you're part of the team, even if you can't be there every day. Distance caregiving poses distinctive problems, but once you've done your homework and worked out any glitches, you can feel you've done your best.

*C*reeping Caregiving – First, you tried to help your elderly neighbor out, well, in neighborly ways— give a hand in the garden, pick up some groceries when she was tired, help her out in the kitchen when the dish pile threatened to collapse from the sheer volume. You also recognized during your clean-up that she's losing weight from not eating regularly. Last month, she asked you to give her a hand with her bills. She couldn't read the small print, anymore. Just this week, she needed assistance getting to her doctor's appointment. She can no longer drive with her failing eyesight, and someone needs to take notes during her doctor's visit, because she can't remember what he said. You're almost afraid what the next phone call will bring. What can you do about this only-too-common case of "caregiver creep?"

Most caregiving begins in small installments—a little help here, a bit more there and before long, you are devoting hours a week that may only too easily turn out to be a major undertaking, and appropriate a huge chunk out of your schedule. Rather than withdrawing altogether from the daily demands of caregiving, try some suggestions for changing a potentially untenable situation.

1. Invite the neighbor, friend or relative who has been imposing on you to your home for lunch or coffee. Open up the conversation to find out their health status, and if family or friends are aware of the situation.

2. Get the names of closest relatives. Contact them as soon as possible to inform them of their

relative's condition, and your ongoing efforts on their behalf. Insist the person(s) visit and determine what level of care their relative may require. Such information usually involves a trained professional to assess the situation appropriately.

3. If the nearest relative(s) lives some distance away, indicate what level of assistance you *can* provide. This may necessitate finding outside help from a reputable agency, such as a home health care agency.

4. Keep the relative informed as changes occur by checking on the elderly person in a discreet manner.

5. If the elderly person is no longer capable of self-care or decision-making, and no relative or friend is available to intervene, consider seeking out help from social services or your local Area Agency on Aging before requesting legal intervention. A *guardian ad litem* could be appointed for someone no longer able to manage their affairs. This is obviously an extreme measure, but may be necessary in certain instances.

FAIR WARNING: Creeping caregiving can happen with neighbors, relatives or friends and catch you unprepared. Assess your comfort level throughout your caregiving, and keep in mind the all-important reality: caregiving may evolve into a total commitment. Know your own limits before you overextend yourself.

Delirium – Complications from routine procedures or a major medical setback can land your loved one in the intensive care unit (ICU). Be prepared for the possibility that your loved one may begin behaving oddly. He or she may experience what's called delirium, a rapidly developing and severe confusion accompanied by altered consciousness and an inability to focus.

Delirium is the most common complication of hospitalization among older people, and almost 80 percent of those treated in ICUs develop it. When this malady isn't recognized, it can hinder recovery. Prolonged delirium is associated with poor long-term outcomes, both mental and physical, and may even lead to death.

Among older people, delirium can be induced by a wide range of conditions: infection, insufficient food and drink, a trauma such as surgery or injury, uncontrolled pain, medications, or simply the unfamiliar surroundings of a hospital.

If your loved one has dementia, he or she is much more likely to develop delirium when hospitalized or even at home. Please note that delirium and dementia are two very different things. Delirium usually arises rapidly, fluctuates in severity and involves changes in consciousness and attention. It also clears up within days or weeks. Dementia, which comes on slowly, is progressive and usually permanent. Until dementia becomes severe, consciousness and attention are still possible.

Here are a few helpful tips for preventing delirium when your loved one is hospitalized.

Families. An engaged and attentive family member can help prevent delirum and advocate for the patient so they receive optimal care. Because family members see their loved one through the entire journey from primary care to hospitalization to rehabilitation, they are the logical advocates for their patient.

Consult with a geriatric specialist. Not all surgeons are familiar with delirium. When an older person plans a hip replacement or any other surgery requiring anesthesia or sedation, advice from a geriatric physician can facilitate planning for medication, pain control, post-operative mobility and sleep support.

Bring a full medication list to any new health professional. Many drugs that act on the brain can cause delirium, including narcotic painkillers, sedatives, stimulants, sleeping pills, antidepressants, Parkinson's disease, medication and anti-psychotics. Even antihistamines and some drugs for digestive problems, allergies and severe asthma can contribute to delirium. Additionally, all medications should be reported because they could interact with drugs given in the hospital.

Make things familiar. Take along a few family photos or comforting objects—a relaxing music CD, a rosary, a favorite blanket—to the hospital. Calm conversations about current events or family activities can be comforting.

Staying close. Family members provide the greatest comfort and reassurance, and are the first to recognize when their family member is behaving inappropriately. Plan to have a family member nearby night and day while the patient is in a state of delirium.

Don't forget sensory aids. Eyeglasses, hearing aids and dentures are often put away during a hospital stay, but that could leave the patient disoriented and less able to function. Be assertive to hospital staff about their use. If concerned about loss, leave an expensive hearing aid at home, and pick up an inexpensive hearing amplifier at an electronics store.

Promote activity. Help your loved one get up and walk two or three times a day. Exercise their brain with conversation, crosswords, card games or other pastimes, depending on their mental ability.

Be there for meals. With companionship and assistance, the patient is far more likely to eat and drink an adequate amount. Be prepared to bring in a favorite food that you know will help to cheer up the patient.

Participate in discharge planning. Patients are sometimes sent home or to a rehabilitation center while still delirious. A patient with delirium cannot fully understand discharge instructions, so family members should be on hand to help—and ask about specific symptoms, indicating that their loved one needs to head back to the hospital. Make certain that nursing staff know your loved one's pre-hospitalization level of functioning, so they won't assume that the current behavior is typical. Ask for a complete medication review. It might be useful to discontinue some medications (such as sedatives) that were added during hospitalization.

*D*ementia – What older person does not fear dementia, a condition that affects over 50 percent of elderly people 85 years and older? Dementia is a general term for a decline in mental ability severe enough to interfere with daily life. While symptoms of dementia can vary greatly, the mental functions most likely to be involved include:

- Ability to focus and pay attention
- Reasoning and judgment
- Visual perception
- Short-term memory loss
- Communication and language

Dementia is caused by damage to brain cells that can be permanent and worsen over time. Certain conditions may improve, though, when the condition is treated and addressed, including depression, medication side effects, sleep deprivation, alcoholism, thyroid problems and vitamin deficiencies. Age and genetics both contribute to the likelihood that an aged person will experience dementia. Alzheimer's disease is one of the most serious causes of dementia with symptoms starting out slowly and gradually getting worse.

Caregivers take heed. When your loved one begins to have problems with short-term memory, keeping track of a purse or wallet, paying bills, planning and preparing meals, remembering appointments or traveling out of the neighborhood, it may be time to act. Intervention early in the dementia process allows your loved one to get the maximum benefit from available treatments. It also allows time to plan for the future when more supervision may be required.

Without underestimating the dreadful effects of advanced dementia, it may be worthwhile to consider a cultural explanation for our collective reaction to this condition. Western societies generally revere the mind, holding cognitive abilities as the measure of the individual. We reward superior mental achievement with public recognition, awards and opportunities. While heroes get their due, the emphasis focuses on materialism: appearance, wealth, power and rational achievement. Even in America, we have very limited standards for full acceptance, and sainthood is not among the qualities we hold dear.

Once a person begins "slipping" in old age—showing signs of "losing it," we throw up our hands in horror. We wonder what comes next, and whether we can handle it. But is it possible we've thrown in the towel too soon without considering another version of the story: a more positive reading of a person with dementia?

Of course, the first job is taking care of your loved

one's physical and safety needs. Once that's done, you can try relaxing and being more playful. You'll find your loved one will join you—or even lead in some cases—in lighthearted pastimes: dancing spontaneously to an inner song, enjoying old family photos, thrilling to the tender touch of a grandchild, smiling to the strains of remembered melodies, nose wrinkling in delight with the fragrance of a summer garden and eye-opening awe at the splendor of a new dawn or the electrifying sight of a canopy of stars.

Personality changes are common with dementia—and sometimes for the better. My friend, Mike Mikkelsen, who recently passed from complications related to advanced Parkinson's disease, remarked: "I think Parkinson's has tenderized me." You can easily see that being alive comes in many different ways.

When you look into the eyes of a person with dementia, you see a full human being, different from the normal, but not less than one. Peer into your loved one's eyes and you can still recognize the inner person, who with all the outer imperfections remains inwardly intact. It's like getting to know someone all over again. Your loved one may even be willing to share the delights of being "differently-abled" with you.

⟨❧⟩

*E*lderly **Drivers** – How should we take away the keys from a loved one whose driving ability has gone from adequate to potentially dangerous? This is one of the most contentious issues confronting caregivers today. For older Americans, driving their car is synonymous with freedom and independence. They're rarely likely to give this up on their own, or at least without a significant struggle.

Bear in mind that the majority of older drivers are safe and free from accidents. Statistics show that elderly people are, in general, very safe drivers, compared with other age groups. The rate of fatal crash involvement has actually decreased for drivers 70 and above in the past two decades. Possible factors contributing to lower risk for elderly drivers include safer vehicles, more defensive driving, and being both more physically fit and healthier than past generations of older adults.

Three trends could raise the risk level for older Americans. In 2007, more than 20 million licensed drivers over the age of 70 were on the road, a number set to increase greatly as the Baby Boomer generation advances. In addition, older people are now driving longer and further, accumulating more miles than they did in the past. More miles means higher risk of accidents. Finally, as the population ages, their capabilities invariably decline.

Vision problems make it difficult to drive, especially at night. Some have hearing impairments to the extent that horns or sirens cannot be heard. Others have mobility issues, such as joint or muscle tightness, making it harder to check mirrors or avoid blind spots. Reaction time also slows for elders as the years take their toll on reflexes, making them slower to respond. Chronic health problems begin to accumulate, including dementia or brain impairment, arthritis, diabetes, stroke and heart failure, among others, which can further reduce focus or limit response time. Drowsiness, often from medications or illness-related insomnia, can seriously impair an older driver.

A grave concern is that older persons are more likely to be seriously hurt in an accident, require hospitalization or die than a younger person involved in the same crash. Caregivers should be aware of the warning signs that shout: **Stay Off The Road**.

- Incompetent driving at night, even if daytime driving is proficient.
- Drastically reduced peripheral vision, even if 20/20 with corrective lenses.
- Struggling to drive at high speeds on the freeway, even if capable of driving well locally at low speeds.

- Erratic driving, such as abrupt lane changes, braking or acceleration, hitting curbs, missing turns or scaring passengers or pedestrians.
- Getting lost frequently, even when driving on familiar roads.
- Trouble reading street signs or navigating directions.
- At-fault accidents or more frequent near-crashes. Look for dents and scrapes on the car, garage doors, mailboxes, fences and curbs—definite signs of trouble.
- Failing to use turn signals or keeping them on without changing lanes.
- Drifting into other lanes or driving on the wrong side of the road.
- Range-of-motion issues, such as failing to look over the shoulder, trouble shifting gears or confusing gas and brake pedals.
- Slower braking response.

Surprisingly, some professionals believe that mild dementia is no longer a reason to take away an elderly person's car keys, according to the newly revised guidelines from the American Academy of Neurology (2010). Not everyone agrees. "A demented person behind the wheel of a vehicle can be equivalent to that person having a loaded weapon" says Dr. Sam Gandy of the Mount Sinai Alzheimer's Disease Research Center. Those "out of control" vehicles, he warns, driven by elderly drivers, are the same ones who plow into crowds of bystanders, one result of ignoring this problem. ABC News reports that red flags for drivers with dementia include "driving fewer miles, collisions, moving violations, avoiding driving at night or in the rain and displays of aggressive or impulsive personality traits."

Not sure how to have that "car key conversation" that caregivers dread? Talking with your elder without a plan may yield little success. Here are some possible options for introducing the topic.

Begin by strongly recommending a fitness program geared to increase response time and mobility if those appear to be the major concerns. If the problem goes deeper, approach your parents' physician about having that all-important driving discussion. But don't expect the doctor to be responsible for your loved one's actions if he or she refuses to take the doctor's advice.

Another option is to check online for various mini-courses. "How To Know When Your Parents Should Stop Driving," "What To Do If Your Parents Refuse To Stop Driving," or "How To Approach Your Parents With Concern About Their Driving" are a few examples of what's available.

Sometimes, the car key conversation simply doesn't work. More extreme measures become necessary. You could disable the vehicle or even remove it altogether. Consider following the advice of some experts and file an unsafe-driver report with your state motor vehicles department, says Jane Gross in *The New York Times*. If you don't wish to take that responsibility, have your doctor send a letter to the department.

Other approaches are far less severe. If you present the elderly driver with some alternatives, it could increase the likelihood that your loved one will give up the keys voluntarily. You can do this by helping them envision life without a car. A conversation that includes the following may make a huge difference.

Know the local transportation alternatives. Public transportation that includes low-cost vans or taxis and other local driving services can accommodate your elder, enabling them to pursue their customary activities.

Investigate local home delivery services. A number of delivery services to your loved one's home may include groceries, dry cleaning and take-out food.

Emphasize monetary savings. Insurance, gasoline, maintenance and repair, registration and licensing add up to thousands of dollars every year. If your loved one is using the car only a few times a week, it could be a big cost saver.

Keep an open mind and be flexible. Allowing seniors to hang on to their car and have others use it to drive them around could reduce their sense of loss greatly. College towns are great places to recruit competent student drivers at reasonable rates.

Check out neighbors and friends for assisting your loved one. Often, when friends or neighbors know that your loved one can no longer drive, they are a first responder for helping to run those errands.

Look for driver safety programs under the auspices of your state motor vehicle licensing department. AAA or AARP driving programs may also be available in your state. Visit keepingussafe.org for additional options in your area.

I recommend *five rules of the road* for caregivers that can lessen a loved one's reaction to retiring from driving:

1. Have a caring, thoughtful plan before opening up the driving conversation.

2. Express your empathy by envisioning how you'd feel in a similar situation. It also helps to have other family members present for the discussion that should be *caring not confronting*.

3. Keep the conversation non-accusatory, honest and between adults, not child and parent. Indicate your concern for safety and well-being. Offer help that goes beyond simply providing rides when needed.

4. Encourage your senior to use positive language to describe their situation to others, and support them in reaching out for assistance.

5. Help your loved one make a weekly schedule that combines trips on days when a caregiver or friend can drive.

❦

F

*F*amilies in Crisis – When we caregivers step up and provide unpaid assistance to our loved ones with chronic diseases or disabilities, it's not only the primary caregiver who juggles work, family and caregiving responsibilities. The *entire* family is seriously impacted by their loved one's incapacities. Profound shifts in family organization and comfort levels can be part of the picture as everyone attempts to respond to this new set of circumstances. The whole family will be more at ease when all members address some crucial caregiving questions *before* their loved one is incapacitated.

1. What are the actual duties and tasks that must be done? How will it impact family members in terms of time, finances, jobs and psychological well-being?

2. Who will be involved? Are all family members expected to pitch in and do their share? What happens to family relationships when one or more members decline to participate? Or, if they participate only reluctantly or with a negative attitude?

3. Where will caregiving occur? Will the older person or couple be obliged to sell their home and move into their adult children's household—or more likely, into institutional care? What about caring for Mom and Dad or a spouse in their own home? Will this require the caregiver to move out of her own home—full or part-time? What about caring for her own family, if a woman has dependent children? How willing are family members to sacrifice their wife and mother for the older generation?

4. What are the financial costs involved? Can the family rely on government and health insurance when facing unexpected medical expenses?

5. What are the often hidden social and psychological costs for the caregiver? For example, how will this impact on the caregiver's marriage, career, relationship with children, friends, community and cherished lifestyle? What kind of services will be needed for their loved one and how can family members contribute to help pay for these expenses?

6. How can family members utilize their strengths and provide relief to the designated caregiver in other ways—respite care (other than family), taking turns giving care, psychological support or other forms of assistance? Can this support be sustained over the course of their loved one's illness?

Because family members are the bedrock of our long-term care system, caregivers need to pay special attention. Everyone can be informed so they're better prepared to embrace the multiplicity of physical, emotional and social tasks that daily care of a disabled person requires. Family members are much more likely to come together to help shoulder the responsibility when they know what the situation involves. The key to a mutually harmonious and satisfactory outcome is knowledge. And we know within our hearts that *knowledge is power*.

$\mathcal{G}$

rowing Costs of Care – The price tag for end-of-life care can be overwhelming for most Americans. According to *Time* (June 11, 2012), skilled nursing facilities, which can provide extensive, ongoing medical care, are the most expensive, with average costs of $222 per day. That's a whopping $6,660 per month. Next in line are assisted living facilities, which offer a home-like atmosphere, and cost $3,300 per month and up for a one-bedroom private residence. A third option, home health care, allows elderly patients to stay in their homes while receiving daily care.

The national median hourly rate for a non-Medicare certified home care aide is $19. Prices vary from state to state on all facilities. For instance, Alaska's skilled nursing facilities charge a median cost of $783 daily, which adds up to an astounding $23,490 per month.

Do we dare explore hospital charges? Amanda Bennett, who chronicles her husband's end-of-life drama in *The Cost of Hope*, indicates just how out-of-control our system really is. In the last year of his life, they paid $33,382 for one hospital stay; $43,711 for the next.

And, a final $14,022 for the last three days of life. Over a seven-year period total, costs for care were an unbelievable $618,616.

Is this an inevitable part of the American way of dying? The word is spreading to patients and their families that these excess expenses are an unfortunate side effect of medical advances and specialization. Our medical system is a dysfunctional one that feels like a hyped-up conveyor belt passing patients from one professional to another. Critics say that the medical machine keeps on ordering tests and procedures even on dying patients, treating the symptoms, but ignoring the whole person. In short, we have a disease-treatment system rather than a health care system caring for human beings, which does little to extend life, and may make matters worse, especially for patients with dementia and their caregivers.

How can patients and their families fight back against overtreatment and runaway costs that may plunge families into bankruptcy and poverty, not to mention emotional turmoil? I recommend three approaches. First is careful monitoring of all tests to avoid duplication. A second consideration is to evaluate your insurance company's payment for specific procedures, which can vary widely. Third is to have that conversation with trusted professionals, your primary physician or hospice worker, about when "enough is enough," and to make an immediate shift into "comfort care." Be certain you have the correct legal documents to ensure your loved one's wishes are followed.

Your calm and supportive presence, along with pain management, can raise everyone's spirits, most significantly your dying loved one's sense of peace.

iring Home Health Care – Just when you think you can handle everything that comes your way—job, teenage kids, friends, looking after mom—you sense your overwhelming fatigue. You realize the time has come to bring in much-needed home health care for your ailing loved one. Finding the right caregiver will be a test of your ingenuity. Some caregivers are phenomenal—they can't give enough. But beating the bushes to find a safe, well-trained caregiver requires some real detective work. Begin by looking for help through word-of-mouth, local agencies and lists of professional caregivers.

Experts say you need to be warned. The person you've hired to look after your aging parent or ill relative can be quite unreliable—untrustworthy, unschooled, uncaring or worse, have a history of abuse. It can be the Wild West out there, so proceed with caution.

Make unannounced visits to the home. Spend a few hours watching how the caregiver interacts with your loved one. Pick up cues to see that your loved one is being fed and cared for. Keep an eye out for weight loss, dirty clothes and urine odors. Remember how you checked up on your kids' babysitters? You'll need to practice the same kind of diligence for your loved one now.

Work with a geriatrician and social worker. They can help identify problems. Ask specifically: "What will my mom need?" "How can I monitor progress of her condition when I can't be there every day?" Don't be upset that you don't know very much about this next phase that you're dealing with. You can learn on the job.

Supervise caregivers. If you're using an agency, make sure it tracks your loved one's care provider frequently at first, and then at least once a month. Find out how it recruits and trains its employees. You'll need to set in motion more regular visits to check up on the situation, especially if your loved one suffers from memory loss. For greater confidence, try interviewing two or three agencies before you make a final decision. Keep in mind, you will need to run a background check and drug screen for any caregiver you hire.

Listen to your intuition. If you hang out long enough with your beloved parent, you can sense when things aren't quite right. Mom appears listless or quiet— not at all like her usual bubbly self. And her appetite has fallen off, too. You ask the doctor about it, but he says, "She's holding her own, just a little depression." Talk to your mom. Ask her specifically "What do you like about your new caregiver?" "What turns you off about her?" "What would you like to see happen?" Don't hesitate. Make that call to the agency if you wind up being unhappy with the one you've got.

Maybe you weren't prepared to do Nancy Drew-like sleuthing when you took on caregiving. When it comes to hiring companions or caregivers, nosing around pays big dividends: safety, comfort and peace of mind.

*H*oliday Caregiving – Finally, the holiday season is here. You've completed all the preparations, the company has arrived, the turkey is in the oven and now you're ready to pick up Mom from the Happy Trails Assisted Living Home. Mom's been living there for about six months—well, at least since her Alzheimer's disease became too progressive to keep her in her own home. Won't she be surprised when her three out-of-town children, their spouses *and all* four of the grandchildren burst onto the scene?

As you and your mom walk in the door, you're assaulted by the grandkids' rap music from the living room, the smell of something burning, every light on in the house—including an overly bright Christmas tree—and suddenly the four darling grandkids come bounding in to welcome Grandma with shrieks of laughter. Grandma's knees buckle and she slowly crumbles to the floor. What went wrong?

You need a holiday survival guide to get you through this, or any other holiday, when your loved one has dementia or Alzheimer's disease. Holidays, birthdays and special occasions can bring mixed emotions for family members caring for aging parents, an ill spouse, relative or family friend. Many family caregivers feel so weary and overwhelmed with daily duties that the thought of "enjoying the occasion" creates only sadness, depression and resentment. Here are a few suggestions to ease the stress of any special event, and turn a potential nightmare into a real celebration.

- Turn down the volume on voices. Avoid TV background sound with no one watching. Instruct all your guests, particularly the children, to give Grandma their soft voices. Help them understand that she can't hear anybody if everyone is talking at once.

- Refrain from having visitors come to the person all at once. Trying to recognize too many faces at once, and the sounds of multiple voices, can be extremely confusing. Avoid over-stimulation and over-tiring by having your loved one eat earlier in the day. Schedule travel plans to avoid long travel for your loved one or back-to-back arrivals and departures for visitors.

- Keep those lighted decorations within bounds. Blinking lights and large holiday displays can leave your loved one feeling less than serene.

- Involve the person in familiar activities, such as sharing blessings or toasts, or even helping with their favorite activities, whether baking cookies, raking leaves, polishing the silver or playing a simple game.

- Include easily recognizable music that's soothing to the person with dementia. Because most people tend to retain vivid musical memories from the past, your best bet is offering traditional holiday music, uplifting choral groups or popular music from the era when they were young. Assist your loved one to locate the right chair so the music will be audible, but not overwhelming.

• Holiday stress can also be reduced by passing on host responsibilities to others. In some cases, having the celebratory gathering at the assisted living or skilled nursing facility can be very helpful for a person with advanced dementia. Sometimes, the facility provides the meal; otherwise, bring your own family favorites. This arrangement avoids both travel and dislocation for the person and keeps the celebration in a familiar environment.

• Gifts should be appropriate for the loved one's dementia level. Dementiatoday.com recommends that for Early Stage Dementia, when individuals may be aware of their problems, choose gifts that enhance independence (tickets to a musical or sporting event), a fruit basket, or family photo albums. Middle Stage Dementia, where more assistance is required, you can try gifts that focus on their mental level of organization. Picture books of historical places, nature or celebrities or taped religious services and music from their former church are just two examples of gifts that work for a person with a short attention span. Late Stage Dementia, when the capacity for comprehension is severely limited, requires uncomplicated and comforting gifts, such as memory boxes made up of old photos and mementos, stuffed animals or dolls, hand and body lotion, lap robes or warm footwear to help circulation.

- Develop your own healthy self-care plan long before the holidays begin. You can get a holiday boost by following some of these tips: Allowing for "good enough"—email those Christmas cards or have your holiday meal catered, if your budget allows. Be *free* from the "shoulds."
  I *should* be happy. I *should* invite my friends over. I *should* carry on my usual holiday plans. Extend compassion to yourself. Take time for regular breaks, meditation and leisure activities. Add special treats to your own holiday gift list—a manicure, a movie, a massage. Plan ahead and ask for help. Rely on professional home care providers to step in and provide a variety of services from respite care and transportation to light housekeeping and meal preparation.

Family caregivers who self-sacrifice and extend love to another need not run themselves ragged from the strain of care at holiday time. Reduce stress by setting priorities and having clear plans for both your loved one and other family members. These sensible tips will free you considerably from the anxiety and stress associated with any holiday.

*H*ospice – When you or someone you know serves as the main support for a very ill person, make sure you include this step—contacting hospice. When medical interventions cannot offer a cure, hospice provides care, comfort and assistance for persons with life-limiting conditions as well as their families. Hospice aims to make the person comfortable and relieve their symptoms and pain for the entire length of their illness.

Not everyone is eligible for hospice. To receive hospice, the ill person's physician must be willing to state that death can be expected within six months if the disease follows its normal course. This does not mean that if the person's life extends beyond six months that hospice will stop treatment. As long as the physician and hospice team certify that conditions remain life-limiting, hospice will continue to provide services.

Hospice is a family-centered team approach that includes a doctor, nurse, social worker, counselor, chaplain, home health aide and trained volunteers. The team works together to focus on the dying person's needs—physical, psychological, social and spiritual. The goal is to help keep the person's pain and symptoms under control, while offering supportive counseling to the patient and family members.

Caregivers will be relieved to know that hospice provides treatment the last months of life, regardless of one's ability to pay. Medicare Hospice Benefit, Medicaid Hospice Benefit and private insurers all reimburse expenses. If a person lacks coverage through these means, hospice will work with the person and their family to ensure services can be provided. Weary caregivers can count on hospice to carry a large part of the load so they can prepare themselves and their family members for their loved one's final days, as well as be ready for the time when they themselves are no longer caregiving.

I

nformation Overload – Do you understand what your doctor is telling you? The overwhelming nature of the Information Age can assault both patient and caregiver when it comes to gathering pertinent information about any medical condition. Recent studies have shown that almost half of all Americans have trouble obtaining, comprehending or acting on information that is important to their health. They suffer from what researchers now call "limited health literacy."

"We are in the midst of a major upheaval," says Dr. Rebecca L. Sudore, Assistant Professor of Medicine at the University of California, San Francisco. "Over the years, the health system has shifted from a paternalistic, doctor-centered model to one that is patient-centered with shared decision-making." In a time when much patient care occurs at home, where patients and their families take responsibility for the largest part of health care, limited health literacy can have devastating consequences.

Elderly patients with limited health literacy are almost twice as likely to die. These patients may not comprehend the severity and complexity of their disease. When persons cannot take care of themselves, it may be that no health professional has spoken to them in a way they can process. Often, pride prevents the older person from asking for help. This leaves caregivers and other family members to sort out all the details of care, including unsolicited advice from every quarter. From Aunt Phoebe to Mary Jones, your next door neighbor, and a myriad of visiting relatives—all have the "solution" for what ails the patient.

Of course, health literacy may not be possible for the very old, disabled, frail or cognitively challenged person. However, caregivers can make it a point to be educated about their loved one's condition, and if the person is capable, communicate this knowledge to their loved one. Here are a few suggestions for caregivers to help themselves and their loved one toward greater health literacy.

- Urge your loved one to learn more about their condition. Many older patients were raised in an era in which it was assumed that the doctor was always right, and so they are likely to accept information even when they don't understand it.

- Choose a primary physician you both can relate to with ease when dealing with multiple health professionals.

- Distinguish between types of practices and hospitals—for example, between smaller community hospitals and large academic hospitals. Typically, a patient sees not only his or her physician at university hospitals, but also medical students, residents and interns. Be clear about who is responsible for your loved one's care. Similarly, differences in medical practices—for example, small versus large; general practice versus specialists—imply that you may not always be interacting with the same physician. Again, locate a doctor who can give you clear and objective information. Many hospitals now hire physicians who only work within the hospital. Hospitalists, as they're called, may create confusion for a patient when the expectation exists that their personal physician will be visiting them. This may not be the case.

Even under the best of circumstances, a host of reasons can prevent you from understanding what a doctor says. Consider how any and all of the following can put you and your loved one in harm's way.

Terminology. Few of us know the correct medical terms for specific conditions. If you didn't know the term, "paradoxical bronchospasm"—a sudden worsening of breathing problems—you could be mystified by the doctor's diagnosis of side effects from certain asthma medications.

Context. You may not understand your loved one's medical situation—how severe an illness may be, or how advanced it is, or which form your loved one may have. You may not be ready when the alarm bell sounds. When Uncle Bill complains about his painful indigestion, should you be aware that he has had chronic heart disease for more than a decade?

Generational Issue. Baby Boomers are often more educated and consumer-oriented than their parents or older relatives. In any "doctor knows best" scenario, it may take more work from you to gain the information you need to make informed choices. Get all the facts you need to be an effective caregiver: Don't be timid about asking for clarification: "Doctor, I'm not sure you explained to Dad how that medicine really works."

Cultural Differences. The doctor or your loved one may be from a culture where patients and family members are not expected to understand the complexity of medical care. Be sensitive, yet persistent, in seeking knowledge to clarify your loved one's condition. If the doctor appears aloof or withdrawn, check with the nurses or other medical staff to clear up any concerns.

Physical or Cognitive Impairments. Functional disabilities may make it very difficult for a patient to read, write, hear and speak. You may require more time to secure information, especially if your loved one prefers to fully participate in the doctor-patient-caregiver interaction. My friend, Carol Schultz, writes about her difficulties in communicating with health providers in *Crossing the Void: My Aphasic Journey.* After her stroke, she lacked the ability to understand medical directives, much less speak on her own behalf. She emphasizes that both caregivers and medical providers for these patients must *always* speak very slowly, enunciate carefully, and watch closely to see that the patient understands what is being said. Carol also pointed out that aphasic patients express themselves differently—eye movements, twitching, guttural sounds or other indications could signal an attempt to communicate.

Emotional Concerns. As a caregiver, you must deal not only with your own anxiety, fear, denial and embarrassment, but also your loved one's sometimes upsetting reactions. This makes it difficult to focus on the information you're being given. If you anticipate a particularly challenging session with the physician—for instance, the doctor tells your mother the cancer has spread to other organs—it may be helpful to bring along a supportive family member or friend to avoid potential confusion about the doctor's opinion. I also recommend taking notes or using a small digital recorder to make sure you're on the right track.

Denial. "I've never felt better in my life," said my husband after the medical team wheeled him into surgery after a heart attack. Unfortunately, his denial severely impeded his treatment and recovery from strokes, and eventually led to his death from heart failure. Hopefully, most patients are not as stubborn and unyielding when they receive a diagnosis. But denial can show up in other behavior. It may involve a refusal to take medicine or follow the doctor's orders. Another denial strategy is to strike out against the doctor or the caregiver: "I'm fine— you're the sick ones. Why not leave me alone?" Isolation and withdrawal can also hide a serious health problem, especially if the person lives alone. As difficult as it may be to deal with denial, you can be on the lookout with older loved ones to ensure that someone is visiting them on a regular basis.

If you think the medical world can be complicated, online medical information and advice can be shocking. With thousands of facts available at the swipe of a finger, how can you decide which information is accurate and relevant to your situation? Facts and figures can be over-abundant and even inaccurate. Consider who is sponsoring the website: a reputable research study or a pharmaceutical company. Despite these concerns, 52 million Americans have searched for health information on the Internet. And 14 million have been deeply influenced by the information they found on the web.

Gathering your own information has both advantages and disadvantages. On the plus side, caregivers and patients who feel better informed may experience less anxiety and have fewer misconceptions. On the down side, caregivers and patients can become completely obsessed with information, increasing both anxiety and fear. Or your loved one can become convinced that the disease is spreading or that collapse and death are imminent. If either the caregiver or patient interprets the vast catalogue of information as predicting impending doom, stress levels can quickly spiral out of control.

To avoid these pitfalls, be aware of the limitations of online research. Guard against unconfirmed health-related information. Try to approach new information with a degree of detachment and a focused eye for objectivity. Keep a skeptical mind, especially for the quick-fix cures. It's always a good idea to check with your physician about medically related matters before you make any decisions.

Ask the doctor to give you any patient education material that specifically relates to your family's situation. Concentrate on better outcomes for your loved one, rather than worst-case scenarios. Finally, make sure your information gathering is a *secondary* goal that serves both you and your loved one, allowing you to focus on care and attention for the patient.

J

Job Issues – To work or not to work while caregiving? That is the question. Obviously, much of your decision will be determined by the physical and psychological needs of your loved one. If your income level is adequate so that you can devote yourself entirely to caregiving, you are one of the more fortunate ones. For most of us, though, the choice of whether to stay on the job remains a difficult, if not agonizing, option. Let's take a closer look at the concerns you face and some possible solutions.

Elder care responsibilities can interfere with paid employment. When it becomes stressful to juggle caregiving activities with work and other family responsibilities, or if work requirements interfere with caregiving tasks, you may wish to consider making changes in your work life. In a recent national survey, one in five retirees left the workforce earlier than planned because of having to care for an ill parent, spouse or other family member.

To avoid losing your livelihood, determine if you can make adjustments in the job, such as arriving late/leaving early or taking time off, cutting back on work hours or changing jobs. If your employer offers little or no access to flexible work options, your choice may narrow down to stopping work entirely.

Before you make that decision, however, you may find your employer willing to work with you. U.S. businesses currently lose up to an estimated $33.6 billion per year in lost productivity from full-time working employees, due to absenteeism, workday distractions, retraining costs, supervisory time, and reductions in hours. They may welcome an effective employee's staying on the job if accommodations can be made for the elderly relative.

Leaving the workforce for full-time caregiving also has its own set of problems, especially financial hardship. Family caregivers may forego earnings and Social Security benefits if they cut back on hours or quit their jobs to give care. In addition, job security, career mobility and employment-related benefits, such as health insurance and retirement contributions, can be severely impacted. Evidence suggests that women who assume the role of caregiver for aging parents in midlife may substantially increase their risk of living in poverty in old age.

When caregiving itself requires that you work to support your loved one and yourself, you may be confronted with a dilemma: which master to serve? Without a regular paycheck coming in, you may jeopardize not only your future, but your essential effectiveness as a caregiver. If this is the case, other issues undoubtedly will emerge if you choose to keep working. Hiring outside help will almost assuredly be required. Moving your loved one into an assisted living or skilled nursing facility could also work. Bear in mind that asking the neighbors or a grandchild to "look in on Granny" is probably not the answer for freeing you up for employment.

The good news is that employers began adding elder care resources to the range of work-family programs. Studies document that implementation of elder care programs can benefit both employers and employees. Employers have found elder care benefits to be a competitive advantage both in new employee recruitment and retention of existing employees. Family-friendly work policies improve worker retention, productivity, stress levels and health among workers. Caregiver referral programs for working caregivers may include on-site support groups, discounted back-up home care for emergency needs and counseling.

An enormous bonus for working caregivers is the U.S. Family and Medical Leave Act (FMLA), which allows for up to 12 weeks of unpaid, job-protected leave each year to enable a worker to care for an immediate family member (in-laws are not included). To qualify a worker must have worked for the business more than 12 months and contributed more than 1,250 hours of work time.

Unfortunately, those employed at small businesses (under 20 employees) and the self-employed cannot qualify for FMLA. In these cases, you can check out assistance through state programs, such as California's "Kin Care" or Hawaii's outstanding family leave benefits. With one in six full-time or part-time employees caring for an elderly or disabled family member, state-instituted family leave benefits may be the wave of the future.

K nowing the Difference Between Long-Term Adult and Child Care

If you're like me, you thought taking care of your aging or disabled loved one would be much like caring for your children. I have raised 6 children and thought, "How hard could it be?" I couldn't have been more wrong. Child care and long-term adult care are two very different species.

Children are a central focus of most social groups, and for many of us, sharing information about the "stages," problems, joys and stresses of childhood and adolescence with our friends (and even strangers) is a common experience. If we're in doubt about a child's behavior, we can tune in to Dr. Phil or pick up a favorite magazine or self-help book.

Where do you turn when you can't figure out why your older sister is so confused? And, have you already noticed that few friends want to discuss your brother's traumatic brain injury (TBI), your mother's Alzheimer's or your husband's Parkinson's disease?

When you have small children, family members often

can't wait to babysit, or help out in some way. Your parents relish the opportunity to enjoy the kids, rekindling the warmth and love that sustained them while they raised you and your siblings. Your brothers and sisters get involved, too—playing ball enthusiastically or going on outings together. Looking after little ones isn't only emotionally satisfying and fun, but it allows us to be playful and feel "young again." We may even be able to relive our own childhoods, if only for a few, fleeting moments.

By no stretch of the imagination can we say that long-term adult care is "fun," nor can you simply turn over caregiving to peripheral relatives, casual friends or helpful neighbors. The demands of care are frequently too exacting or difficult. Your grandmother needs assistance using the toilet, while your grandfather needs help with the morning routine of washing, dressing, shaving and hair combing. Both require medications to be dispensed at different intervals. And, let's talk about complicated when you add dementia and depression into the mix.

Healthy children follow an upward track: growth and development over time is inspiring to behold. Each of our children has his or her own special destiny, and we strive to promote the best attributes of our offspring: first steps, first words, first day of school, graduation and good job. We can look forward to our children marrying and having families of their own. Typically, we know what to expect.

None of these positive conditions prevail for long-term adult care or for parents whose children have terminal illnesses. Here, the spiral slopes downward and out. Sadly, it's only a matter of time before your loved one deteriorates further and is gone.

You know where the road ends for him or her. Your journey may have only just begun.

L

oneliness – Liv Ullman, the Swedish actress, has said about her relationship with acclaimed film director Ingmar Bergman, "I just think that sometimes it is less hard to wake up feeling lonely when you are alone than to wake up feeling lonely when you are with someone." Caregivers know what it is to be alone with their charge and lonely in the midst of giving care and comfort to another. But what is the difference between alone and lonely? Although we tend to associate being alone with lonely, they're really two distinct realities.

When you live by yourself, you are often solitary, on your own and unaccompanied in life's journey by a beloved other. Once you discover the inner joys of being alone, you'll find that loneliness is not necessarily a part of the picture. You can reach out to others on your own terms. When you share your life with someone you cannot communicate openly and honestly with, or when that person is emotionally distant or unavailable, you can, indeed, feel lonely. However, loneliness is more than a state of mind. It can be a life-threatening condition with major consequences.

Chronic loneliness has two profound effects: biochemical and behavioral. Not only does it trigger an unhealthy immune response, the body's first line of defense against illness. Isolation also raises levels of stress hormones and increases the inflammatory response that, over the long-term, can promote cardiovascular disease, arthritis, cancer and brain degeneration.

Add to this, loneliness undermines people's ability to self-regulate. University of Chicago research demonstrates that lonely individuals tend to do whatever they can to make themselves feel better, if only for the moment. They may overeat, drink too much, smoke, speed or engage in indiscriminate sex. In time, those who are older and lonely are more likely to develop difficulties performing activities of daily living like bathing and dressing, using their arms and shoulders, climbing stairs and walking.

Even more serious, British researchers found recently that social isolation could dramatically increase the possibility of dying for older men and women. Michelle Mitchell, director general of Age UK, said: "This study shows more clearly than before that being lonely and isolated is not only miserable, it is a real health risk, increasing the risk of early death."

If you are a caregiver, it's not possible to talk yourself out of being lonely. No magic wand will make this deep ache disappear. Direct action is necessary to relieve the sense of foreboding and anguish. Many people are tempted to use Facebook and other social media to stave off those lonely feelings. But these are not replacements for face-to-face social contact with relatives and friends.

Recognize how easy it is to become isolated and detached from others when caregiving a cognitively disabled person. Sometimes, it can almost feel as though you and your care receiver are on a remote island completely cut off from everyone. When you've reached this point, you've already gone too far.

Breaking the isolation requires three major shifts. First, reach out to other individuals, who can help you reconnect to outside activities and people. This could be a neighbor, friend, relative or pastor. Second, find a sustaining group that can refuel you emotionally and spiritually. This could run the gamut from a needlepoint sewing circle to a weekly lunch bunch or a caregiver support group. You could also seek out activities that help others while fostering social contacts, like volunteering in a soup kitchen, reading to the blind or assisting in a classroom. Such actions can result in what research shows is a "helper's high."

Third, make arrangements at home for you to take a break from caregiving without feeling guilty or harried. Remember: It is one thing to revel in your aloneness when you are independent or even a solitary person and no one depends upon you. But in the world of caregiving, we are the world to that dependent person. To keep both you and your loved one intact, break free of that isolation, and join up with people and pursuits that make you feel truly alive. A final point: The quality of relationships you make—how meaningful they are to you—counts more than quantity in preventing loneliness.

Let us keep in mind Paul Tillich's wise words, when he said, "Language… has created the word 'loneliness' to express the pain of being alone. And it has created the word 'solitude' to express the glory of being alone."

*L*ong-Distance Caregiving – You may live a mere five miles away from the person needing help or across the country, but the situation remains the same. Caring for your loved one is *further* complicated by travel and logistics.

Long-distance caregiving is a growing trend with challenging problems for adult children. The Pew Research Center estimates that one out of every eight adults in America between the ages of 40 and 60 is both raising children *and* tending to aging parents. Additionally, seven to 10 million adults care for their parents from afar. In a 2004 MetLife study, the average distance for respondents was 450 miles, and nearly a quarter of those surveyed said they were their loved ones' *only* caregiver.

Every phase of caregiving becomes knotty, subject to twists and turns—over the simplest issue. Caring for elderly parents when you can't be with them every day can cause you endless stress and worry. Undoubtedly, you'll be asking some questions.

How can I help my parents decide when it's time to move to a safer, more manageable living arrangement? How can I know what their medical condition really is when each time I call they insist, "I'm just fine?" How can I understand what kind of medical care they're getting in the first place? How can I find local, professional help when they need more assistance? How can I assist my sister who's looking after Mom and Dad without family support?

Distance caregivers often have guilty feelings about not doing enough. The real headache is that you can't take time away from work or leave the family, let alone shoulder the costs associated with travel.

Frank Samson recommends a step-by-step guide for families to cope with long-distance caregiving. Setting up a care plan is the first priority.

- Determine the physical condition of your loved one. How capable are they in terms of managing cooking, shopping, laundry and other everyday tasks?

- Assess the condition of the home environment. Does this work for your loved one's capacities and functions?

- Develop a care team. Talk with the doctor and get recommendations for community resources and support groups. Get local relatives, friends and neighbors to drop in regularly, and give you reports of your loved one's progress.

- Hold a family meeting. Conference calls ease the difficulty of communication, along with texting, video chatting and Facebook. Face-to-face talking may be ideal, but coordination through regular conference calls can do the job. The local caregiver would be the most logical person to keep everyone informed if there's been an accident or medical setback.

- Access local agencies for part-time help or nursing assistance. Much of this can be handled by phone or email. Help and guidance is often just a phone call away.
- Consider the benefit of occasional visits to give joy to your ailing relative, and obtain a more accurate picture of the situation.
- Regular calls, emails and snail mail can also keep you in touch without the necessity of travel.

Fortunately, technology can be there even when you can't. If the person shows signs of physical weakness, ignores once-common tasks and personal grooming or is becoming generally more forgetful, it may be time for a medical alert device. Other options include remote monitoring and real-time Web-based home health systems, complete with daily reports, records management and alerts in the event of an emergency.

We've all known people who let guilt about not being with a loved one all the time keep them from doing very helpful, useful things. When you do whatever you can and you do it from the heart, it will ease your concerns about your care receiver's well-being.

M

Managing **Chronic Care** – Chronic care is by its nature long term, and the training and supports for family caregivers to manage this care must be of similar duration. In a recent AARP publication, *Home Alone: Family Caregivers Providing Complex Chronic Care*, you can discover *what* is involved, *how* to accomplish this, and *why* your involvement is so significant for both you and the care receiver. Let's review some major points.

What is involved in caring for a sick elderly family member or friend can be overwhelming, and entails four distinct functions: normal household tasks, personal care, managing medications and even medical/nursing tasks. Let's look at each function. Household tasks can mount up quickly—handling the cleaning, laundry, cooking, grocery shopping, meal preparation and finances are just the beginning. Add to this the personal care of your frail loved one—bathing, toileting and eating. Transferring or moving the patient from bed to toilet or wheelchair to bed/toilet often becomes necessary with a major injury or at the end of life. Of course, personal care also consists of all the loving interaction and assistance you provide.

Nowadays, medication management is no longer a cobbled together process. Instead, your loved one may require anywhere from five to nine medications daily (but sometimes more) that must be administered at specific times, day and night. Interactions between different drugs are all too common, so you have to watch carefully for possible side effects. You should notify the patient's physician immediately if distinct physical, emotional or behavioral changes occur.

Medical/nursing tasks involve an entirely new array of duties, including wound tending, helping with assistive devices (canes or walkers), preparing food for special diets, delivering intravenous fluids and injections, using meters or monitors (e.g., blood pressure or glucometer), and operating durable medical equipment (e.g., hospital beds, lifts, wheelchairs). As few as ten years ago, these tasks were nearly all confined to trained nurses or physicians. Today, with the expanding older population and hospital costs, family caregivers are increasingly taking over these responsibilities.

How you accomplish this requires—no surprise—training by medical professionals. To avoid the pitfalls of caregiving—feeling overwhelmed, unsure of yourself or depressed—you *can* learn to administer drugs and to carry out medical/nursing care tasks. Before bringing your loved one home from the hospital or rehabilitation center, make a point to work with available medical professionals. Your doctor, facility nurse, social worker or occupational therapist can show you the ropes in a systematic way. Once your patient is home, have a trained person who is well-versed in home care to go over these new routines with you.

Why your involvement is so crucial to both you and your loved one is the greater ease and confidence both you and your loved one can have. Additionally, home care for the physically and cognitively disabled is very *special* care, as it nurtures the bond between you. Your participation in care also prevents or postpones skilled nursing care, which can be outrageously expensive and invariably less personal.

Being prepared for the worst, but trained for the best outcome—that is half the battle. The other half involves organizing your care duties without forgetting about *yourself* (see *The ABCs of Caregiving: Words to Inspire You*).

Skilled Nursing and Residential Care

Residential care includes assisted living, family group homes and skilled nursing facilities. You can work wonders with advocacy *after* a person has entered a residential facility. But what about the time *before* the elder's need for help is sudden and obvious. You may need to do your homework earlier than you planned.

Check for quality—that's your first and foremost task. Loved ones do immensely better when they live in a facility near to cherished persons, places and things—family, friends or community activity. Sometimes, though, you may have to go further afield to locate a good one.

Evaluate a residential facility by scheduling a tour. Ask the manager how the facility addresses your loved one's specific and changing needs. Be sure to make unscheduled visits. Ask residents what they do during the day and what they enjoy about the community. Develop a list of your top choices and survey these facilities. Will your loved one be more comfortable in one setting compared with another?

Inspect state licensing requirements with the department of health. Also, ask about accreditation with your Area Agency on Aging. Inquire about any reported complaints with the appropriate state agency. Talk with a geriatric care management company about which facility level your loved one needs. Assisted living offers more limited care, but typically has more independent living arrangements. Elder care lawyers and other professionals may also offer tips on top rated facilities.

Get your loved one on board. Ease into it if possible. Transitioning from home to a care center can be quite painful for you and your loved one. You could start with hiring a cleaning person, getting them accustomed to outside help. Try presenting care in whatever form and try it out for a while.

Set a time line. Get your own assessment of your loved one's needs and abilities for better placement. Assessments can be arranged through both nonprofit groups or private professionals. Try to arrange for the least restrictive environment. For example, if your loved one can manage most activities of daily living in her own home, but can no longer cook, you could bring food in or set up a meal program with a local agency. When it's apparent your elder can no longer manage in his or her own home, be prepared to take that next step.

Fine-tune your language. Frame the move in terms of what is most appealing to your loved one. Perhaps it's a deserved luxury. Maybe it's something recommended by a trusted friend or doctor. You could even promote it in terms of cuisine or social activities.

Don't command. When you act like a boss, you will get resistance, warns Linda Fodrini-Johnson, executive director of Eldercare Services. Include your loved one in all decisions, and avoid making blanket statements about what they "need to do." Other strategies prevail for your cognitively disabled senior, as well. I recommend a consultation with a dementia expert.

Seek answers. If your loved one is reluctant to accept care, try to figure out why. You may be operating with one scenario, while they're working with an entirely different picture. After you've done that initial groundwork and chosen two or three favorite facilities, offer to go with your loved one to have a tour and meal at each one. Management regularly has open house and dinner invitations. Discuss the pluses and minuses and then make a mutually agreed-upon selection.

Turn the Tables. Emphasize how it eases your fears and helps *you* feel less stressed to know they're in a safe place.

Skilled nursing facilities are no longer the sole answer

to a faltering senior. But it's important to know *when* your loved one is ready for a more secure facility that provides a broad range of nursing care and rehabilitation services.

*M*ild **Cognitive Impairment** – Your loved one forgets someone's name, where he put his car keys, today's date. If memory is becoming troublesome and forgetfulness is happening more and more, it could signal Mild Cognitive Impairment (MCI).

Unlike full-blown Alzheimer's disease or advanced dementia, MCI is a slight, but noticeable, change in thinking and memory skills. In certain cases, it mimics Alzheimer's disease, as symptoms increase over time, which indicates that the same areas of the brain may be affected. MCI is *not* an illness, but rather a *cluster* of symptoms that describe changes in thinking, processing information and problem-solving. Currently, 44 million people in the world have dementia, a condition that affects men more than women.

Bear in mind that mental abilities decline with age, even without dementia or other neurological conditions that affect brain functioning. While the mechanisms for brain change are not fully understood, studies show that the older brain does not work the same as a younger one. The first thing that changes is *processing speed*. As this function slows down, it may seem that the memory becomes worse, but it only means that the same processes take longer than they once did. Verbal ability and spatial abilities also start a downturn, somewhere between six and eight years before death. Illness compounds the effects of age, and contributes to increased mental decline. Caregivers, take notice if the following experience becomes a habit: "*Dad called me today again because he can't remember his next doctor's appointment, where his schedule book is or when he's supposed to take his new medication.*"

In addition, keep an eye out for some other common symptoms.

Typical Symptoms

- More frequent difficulty remembering simple things.
- Harder to follow a conversation or instruction.
- Regularly losing his train of thought.
- Feeling overwhelmed when attempting to make plans or decisions.
- Losing his way even in familiar locations.
- Secondary emotional symptoms, such as depression, anxiety, irritability or apathy.

However mild the cognitive decline, it definitely affects the ability to work, earn money, keep up with driving and regular daily activities, as well as remain independent. Caregivers may wish to step in when more serious declines show up. It bears repeating that when your loved one begins missing appointments, losing things frequently, having difficulty remembering dates, places and names—these can all point to MCI.

Another serious consideration: MCI often impairs a

person's ability to interact with the visual world, including finding their way home, and judging distance and timing behind the wheel. What can a caregiver do?

For early MCI, help him locate a global positioning system (GPS) for the car. Urge him to avoid driving during high-traffic times and bad weather. If you have reason to be concerned about his visual acuity, seek an evaluation with your eye doctor. Driving schools or local department of motor vehicles may be able to recommend a specialist to determine if driving is a safe option.

Language and social cognition can become a daily challenge, with a decline in the ability to recall words and use them properly in sentences. Although it takes effort to remember someone's name, share experiences or bolster meaningful conversation, it is assuredly worth the effort. Research suggests that maintaining social interaction is most beneficial for preserving cognition. Urge your loved one to continue to schedule pleasurable activities—dancing, a theater visit, a walk in the park, attending a meeting—that involve interaction with others. Help him to stay positive by suggesting he could lighten up a bit. Humor wins every time—even those memory lapses can be shrugged off as having a "senior moment."

Causes of MCI

- Being 65 or older.
- Having a family history of MCI, Alzheimer's disease or another form of dementia.

- Having certain medical conditions, such as high blood pressure, diabetes, strokes, high cholesterol or heart disease.
- Substance abuse or alcohol abuse.
- Lack of exercise.
- Other causes include: medication interaction, infections, malnutrition, vitamin shortages, thyroid and other metabolic disturbances.

More recent research indicates that a weakened immune system may be a key player in the development of dementia. Whatever the source, cognitive impairment can make even the most positive person feel frustrated. *The Harvard Health Letter* recommends that "good habits, simplified choices and memory tools" can assist mental health greatly. *Dementia Today* provides a number of techniques to help compensate for any memory decline that interferes with your loved one's enjoyment of life, social effectiveness, relationships and goals for the future.

- Be more patient with your loved one, and also ask them to be more patient with themselves. Understand that this condition creates a great deal of frustration, anxiety or sadness, once a person recognizes there has been a significant loss of memory. Persuade the person to slow down, which can sometimes make it easier to remember or complete a task.
- Learn more about MCI and share that knowledge with your loved one and other family members.

This will enable them to better understand the changes they can expect.

- Discuss with your loved one his or her preferences for important decisions, should the MCI progress to dementia.

- Help your loved one find constructive ways to release any anger and frustration. Talking with a close friend or a counselor or joining a support group for people with memory loss can make an enormous difference. The Alzheimer's Association has support groups for people with early onset Alzheimer's, including people with an MCI diagnosis. It can be immensely beneficial to talk to others going through the same experience, or one that is similar. Encourage family members and other care support persons to seek out counseling and support to meet their own needs to better assist their care receiver.

- Continue to explore ways to fulfill needs for intimacy and closeness. Encourage participation in family events and keeping in touch with friends. The desire for close relationships with others continues throughout life.

- Ask your physician for an exercise program that best fits the loved one's needs. Exercise contributes to good physical health, reduces stress, and helps keep the brain as healthy as possible.

- Use visible and/or accessible reminders. Useful strategies your loved one can carry out include

writing notes to himself, posting a large calendar
to track appointments, leaving messages on his
voice mail, using an automatic dispensing pill
box and setting the alarm on a mobile device to
remind him of upcoming events.

- Assist in documenting his or her personal story by
creating a scrapbook, recording special events or
writing their life story. This is a wonderful way to
reflect on life and share with those closest to him
or her. Children and grandchildren will treasure
these keepsakes.

- Keep the disabled mind active by supporting
enjoyable things: working on puzzles, reading
the newspaper, playing cards, listening to music,
writing in a journal, and especially, learning about
something new.

- Know that your loved one is more than someone
with MCI. Celebrate the many and varied
personal attributes the person possesses.

- Increase your awareness of MCI research projects
and consider having your loved one participate in
a medication trial if the physician thinks it might
be helpful.

- Find other ways of reaching out with MCI, such
as becoming an advocate for your loved one and
other individuals. Writing letters and making
phone calls to local and state representatives could
be useful, as could assisting community agencies
in training staff and professionals about MCI.

- Even before your loved one has a diagnosis of
  MCI, a wise move is to complete an Advance
  Healthcare Directive, a Durable Power of
  Attorney and Durable Power of Attorney for
  Finances. These documents will outline the type
  of care he wants and needs in the future, should
  he be unable to state those preferences. Meet with
  a lawyer knowledgeable about estate planning to
  draft a will, set up a trust or handle other related
  legal matters.

Above all, urge your loved one to focus on present abilities and competencies, rather than worrying about what
might happen in the future. Let them know that there
are many ways to live an active and productive life. Best
advice: put the emphasis on what the person *can* do, not
on what he or she can't.

*N*utrition and Health – Have you felt tired lately, just dragging through one day after another? Have you ever considered what you're eating or not eating could be the culprit? Could be, you've been far too busy with your loved one and your other duties to take care of yourself. If you care enough about keeping up your strength, are you willing to try a different approach to give you back some of your old vim and vigor?

"C'mon, eat happy," authors Tyler Graham and Drew Ramsey, M.D. emphasize. Join the millions of Americans who are voting with their feet and walking away from unhealthy and life-threatening diets. Especially keep in mind that a whole-food, plant-based pattern of eating can not only lower your risk for certain diseases. It can reverse their progression. But don't forget to keep some of that comfort food for yourself when the going gets too tough.

Here are the basic 10 food points nutritionists say can get you on the path for happy living.

1. **Build muscle with lean protein** to keep your weight in balance. Cooking with olive oil and

canola oil helps, as well.

2. **Give your brain a youthful boost** with legumes, including beans, and other healthful foods, like white meat turkey, fish and grains.

3. **Get that zest back in your life** by cutting down or eliminating sugar. Reducing your sugar can also ease achy joints.

4. **Gain added energy and reduce your weight** by eating more whole grains and nuts.

5. **Fight harmful free radicals** that cause chronic disease by eating more high fiber foods.

6. **Control your insulin**, blood glucose, cholesterol, cortisol (stress hormone) and mood by eating smaller helpings of food more often.

7. **Stay alert** by avoiding overeating. The hormone cholecystokinin (CCK) can trigger sleepiness.

8. **Regulate your food cravings** by eating breakfast within an hour or so of getting up.

9. **Escape flatulence and inflammation** by staying clear of dairy products.

10. **Control dehydration** by consuming six glasses of fluids a day. And add additional water to balance the drying effect of alcohol or caffeine drinks.

Even adopting a few new food habits can start you feeling more energized. You can begin by cutting back on certain food items, like processed food and red meat, and still keep some of those favorite goodies in your cupboard—like that yummy dark chocolate bar.

O

*O*bstacles to Moving Your Loved One Into Placement – Mary Jones, 77, has been caring for John, her 80 year-old-husband, for more than six years. As John's Parkinson's disease worsens, Mary's stress level rises. She continues to drive herself, day and night, but she's finding it extremely difficult to keep up with his physical and emotional needs. Even more serious, Mary recently has had a series of accidents. Three weeks ago, she had a fender bender that left her badly shaken. Last week, a fall in her kitchen badly bruised her knees. And yesterday, a dangerous slip on her icy front steps sent her to the doctor with three fractured ribs. What's happening with Mary and her resolve to take care of John until his dying day?

Mary represents the millions of women and growing number of male caregivers confronting a common situation. Her loved one requires more intensive care, but she lacks the knowledge, experience, time, energy and money to pursue help. She realizes her stress level is out of control, but she has not yet reached out to family members or friends to assist her with hands-on care. Isolated, overwhelmed and overcome, Mary may need to seriously consider an institutional setting for her loved one.

The caregiver shouldn't wait until she is at the end of her rope. Once the situation begins to look dire, she may want to consider checking out local facilities and determining the different levels of care available, such as skilled nursing, assisted living or family group home. Caregivers face a host of circumstances that can hinder a smooth shift into residential care, however.

1. **The Nature of the Caregiver.** First and foremost is the caregiver herself, and her reluctance to turn over care to others. We can attribute this to the "AAA dilemma of caregivers," a term coined by Linda Burhans, caregiver advocate and author of *Good Night and God Bless.* Caregivers do not ASK for help, they do not ACCEPT help, and they do not ACKNOWLEDGE the help they provide. Asking for, accepting help and acknowledging that you are a deserving person are initial steps for moving forward or even survival. Statistically, caregivers are more likely to die *before* their care receiver.

2. **Procrastination.** Postponing the inevitable appears to be a common issue among caregivers. Postponement requires no decisions be made and no change need occur. Life can continue in its normal round without the caregiver having to make any hard choices. Sometimes, we wait so long that by the time we come around to making

the decision, the patient is near death. The caregiver may not be far behind.

3. **Resistance from Family Members.** A major obstacle for assisting the caregiver in placing her loved one remains the out-of-sight, out-of-mind family member—the one who has had little contact with parents or siblings over the years. Once they're told that a parent must be moved into care, they may act shocked that their loved one will be "dumped" into an institution. Feelings run very high around these issues. Caregivers really have to take the leadership when detractors come along, as they invariably will. Be prepared: One of the more critical detractors could be the care receiver himself. For the World War II generation, the "old folks" home—and this includes any residential setting—represents the last stop before the inevitable end.

4. **Lack of affordability**. The primary reason most working and middle class families continue to provide home care is the high cost of skilled nursing facilities. Americans are currently spending $15 billion a year for residential health care. For the individual consumer, this boils down to some hefty costs.

According to the *Genworth 2013 Cost of Care Survey*, based on 15,000 long-term care providers across the United States, the median annual rate for a resident of an assisted living community is $41,000. The annual amount for a private room at a skilled nursing facility is $83,950, while a semi-private room is $75,405. Nursing facility costs exceed the reach of many already struggling to keep their heads above water. For this reason, many families choose a family group home with fewer number of residents and considerably lower costs.

Adding to the confusion of correct placement is the prospect of exploring funding options through the maze of Medicare, Medicaid, Veteran's Administration and insurance companies, which can be utterly daunting. Caregivers may need assistance from elder lawyers or accountants with making sound financial decisions, including the "spend-down" feature that Medicaid requires before families can expect financial relief.

5. **Psychological Strategies**. Caregivers convince themselves to keep doing what they've been doing, even if it's not working. Fear of change is a major issue for caregivers, which has its source in guilt ("she's sick and I'm still healthy"). When guilt drives persons into caring for others, it generates a negative cycle: the greater the guilt, the more intense the fear. Caregivers often believe that if they relinquish control, it's all downhill from there. The loved one will decline and die. End of story. Not far beyond fear lie denial and avoidance. Denial is eyes closed tightly, therefore not seeing the elephant in the room. Avoidance is eyes open, but an unwillingness to face the truth.

I found the Area Agency on Aging to be the first stop in

my quest for information. Ask personnel at your regional office about recommending a staff member to help sort out various federal, state and local programs. They will undoubtedly guide you to the appropriate support groups and counseling, as well as legal and financial professionals in your community.

Additionally, your personal physician can offer reinforcement for making sound decisions and provide advice for families when it's finally time for the elder to transition into a care facility.

*O*mbudsman – The Ombudsman Program is an important protective service for seniors and their families and serves the public by reviewing and investigating complaints about a certain type of institution or care. You'll be happy to know an ombudsman watches over long-term care facilities for the elderly, such as assisted living, group family homes and skilled nursing facilities. Ombudsmen also advocate on behalf of long-term care residents in general. More than 500 ombudsmen serve in these capacities in all 50 states, the District of Columbia, Puerto Rico and Guam under the authorization of the Older Americans Act. In 2010 Congress funded over $87 million dollars, which also includes people with medical needs living at home.

If you have serious complaints about your loved one's care in a facility and direct communication with the staff has failed, don't hesitate to contact an *ombudsman*. If a person faces immediate danger, such as abuse or neglect, including residents abusing each other, contact the police immediately. Many seniors hesitate to tell their family they are having difficulties, so be on the alert for sudden changes in behavior unrelated to the illness.

Ombudsmen include both volunteers and paid advocates. They work to resolve problems of individual residents, and to bring about changes at the local, state and national levels that will improve residents' care and quality of life. Ombudsmen can do much to improve the living conditions of the elderly and ensure that they receive proper care. With the help of prompt and detailed complaints, ombudsmen can do their jobs effectively.

Occasionally, complaints to an ombudsman fail to adequately resolve a serious problem, but families shouldn't give up. Government licensing agencies and other regulators also accept complaints about problems with long-term care. Another option involves speaking with an attorney. If mistreatment has already caused physical, emotional or financial harm, a lawsuit may be warranted. Change is possible, but it's important that families understand residents' rights, and intervene when their loved one's rights have been violated or they have been harmed while under care. (See also Advocacy.)

P

*P*ain Management – "Take two aspirin and call me in the morning," could well be in order for the occasional indisposition. It barely begins to cover the intricacies of pain management with chronic diseases or end-of-life suffering. In the U.S., more than 100 million people deal with chronic, under-treated pain.

As a caregiver, your ability to address pain management is crucial, whether during your loved one's illness or at the end of life. After all, pain is not only unpleasant, it can threaten a person's well-being, functional ability and quality of life. Chronic pain contributes to interrupted sleep, problem focusing, fatigue and emotional disturbances, such as isolation, depression and worry. And pain is expensive. People with pain use more health care services at greater cost to society.

When Seniors Confront Chronic Pain

Studies estimate that up to 88% of seniors report chronic pain, requiring some form of pain medication. Joint and muscle wear and tear head the list, but other types of chronic pain seniors experience include: arthritis, peripheral neuropathy, central pain syndrome (associated with stroke), repetitive strain injury, lingering pain from injuries or surgery, cancer pain, and depression-related pain.

Chronic pain in seniors can be more challenging both to diagnose and treat than for other age groups, leaving the elder more vulnerable to anxiety and depression. Older adults are also less likely to be forthcoming about their pain, because of generational differences and reluctance to appear vulnerable. They may believe that they should remain stoic and "keep a stiff upper lip." Some may have more trouble communicating their pain because of decreased hearing, compromised abilities associated with a stroke or even dementia.

Treating the pain of older adults, who often have more than one medical condition, can be especially difficult. A large number of older persons suffer from heart disease, lung disorders, diabetes or high blood pressure, each of which requires a cornucopia of medications, further contributing to potential side effects. Adverse reactions from pain medications are more likely to afflict seniors, leading to falls and more damage and complications.

Helping seniors cope with chronic pain may require modest changes, such as a low-impact exercise program, using assistive devices (walker or cane), following doctor's medication instructions to the letter and getting support from friends and other family members.

What else can be done when your loved one has chronic or persistent pain?

Consult your physician or health care organization. Keep in mind that specialists, such as cardiologists or oncologists, are trained to treat illness, not pain. You may need to seek a pain specialist or pain clinic. Fighting pain is so significant that The Joint Commission introduced new standards that require all health care facilities to identify and manage pain effectively. Many institutions now include pain as the fifth vital sign in their care of patients, adding to temperature, blood pressure, pulse and respiratory rate.

Develop a check list with details to take to their doctor. Ask your loved one these questions before your doctor's appointment, and take notes on how they answer.

- When did the pain start?
- What works and what does not work in terms of the treatment thus far?
- Is the pain constant or occasional?
- What words best describe the pain: dull, stabbing, throbbing, aching, pounding?
- What relieves the pain, if anything, and what makes it worse?
- How is the pain affecting your quality of life?

Maintain a record of pain experienced throughout the day. Keeping track of pain throughout the day will help doctors know if the medication levels are right. Have your loved one rate his or her pain from zero (no pain) to 10 (unbearable pain) at different times of the day. If he or she is unable, do your best to track it yourself.

Make a note of what eases the pain (medication, rest or visits) and what makes it worse (lack of sleep, overexertion or stress).

If pain levels are not relieved with medication, go back to the doctor, and have the dosage changed or switch medications. Expect medication amounts to increase as the illness progresses or at the end of life. Different types and levels of pain medication may be required for palliative (chronic) care, when the patient is still active, and comfort care, when the patient is actively dying.

Pain management is partly about prevention. Like many health issues, pain is easier to prevent than to treat. Understand your doctor's orders for medication: frequency, dose and type. Be sure your loved one is taking the medication at the appropriate time. If relief is still not forthcoming, consult the doctor. Make certain your loved one is assertive and tells the doctor that he or she will not tolerate under-treated pain. Be an advocate for your loved one when he or she is not able to speak for themselves. Another point: Be sure to have ample supplies of medication on hand for holidays, weekends and emergencies.

Ask to speak to the medical director or nursing supervisor. This may become necessary if medical staff fail to address your loved one's pain. When your loved one has been hospitalized, is in a facility or under hospice care, make the pain known to staff. Follow up to ensure that the pain has been controlled. Even though facilities no longer can use "chemical restraint," which is the use of painkillers to "quiet" patients, be on the alert for overmedication in skilled nursing settings.

Seriously ill people need special care. Palliative medicine can help. Palliative care is about making the most of life with a serious illness, whether the illness is terminal or not. It focuses on a team approach to helping patients manage their pain and nausea, getting much-needed support and navigating the health care system.

A Typical Patient

John, age 78, had two heart attacks in quick succession and was later afflicted with a series of strokes requiring a complex array of medications to keep him stable. Rather than enhancing John's quality of life, this variety of medications, combined with cardiovascular disease, led to his being incapacitated by persistent pain and severe depression. He was left isolated and indifferent to his fate. His caregiver wife, Anne, desperate to find a solution, sought psychiatric and pharmacological remedies, but met with little success.

Once John was placed in a skilled nursing facility, a neurologist was called in as a last ditch effort to provide relief. Oxycodone (Oxycontin) appeared to be the drug of choice, but side effects were extreme: hallucinations, aggression and bizarre behavior, including being spacy and disconnected. Unable to reach the doctor or convince the nursing staff to discontinue the drug, Anne went to the facility's medical director for help. Yet, it was not until Hospice stepped in with comfort care about a year later did the pain symptoms and depression lessen.

This all-too-common situation offers several important lessons.

- *Medications vary in their effects for different individuals.* People with persistent physical pain or mental anguish need comprehensive and individualized care. This requires early intervention and systematic assessment, monitoring and adjustment of the medications to reduce symptoms and minimize side effects throughout the illness. *Pain medications should be monitored for adverse personality and mood changes as well as physical ones.*

- *Minimum dosages are recommended, although levels of medication depend on the degree of pain, plain and simple.*

- *For people who take opioids (morphine and oxycodone are among them), the body takes a few days to adjust to the medication.* Short-term reactions may be present, such as mental fogginess, sleeplessness, constipation and itchy skin. These side effects are usually temporary. Anyone taking an opioid should keep in close touch with the prescribing doctor to report these short-term effects, many of which are treatable.

- *People often consider pain part of their illness and believe they must learn to live with it.* This prevents them from seeking proper pain management and results in needless suffering. Fears about addiction also inhibit patients from seeking medication.

Long-term chronic and end-of-life conditions typically necessitate pain medication to ease patients' distress. Bear in mind, though, that you cannot force medication on someone who chooses not to take it.

- *In our medication-overload culture, it is useful to understand that drug dependence and addiction are two separate entities.* When faced with serious illness that causes unremitting pain, dependence on opioid-based medications is natural, normal and may not be a problem as long as withdrawal from the medication is done gently under a physician's supervision. Addiction is another thing entirely, and can readily affect people treated for pain. Yet, some people with chronic pain take opioids for years with few side effects.

Other Approaches

When dealing with patients for whom standard pain medications provide poor or inadequate relief, medical providers increasingly are turning to alternative approaches. These run the gamut from exercise, physical therapy, chiropractic treatments, acupuncture, imagery, massage, Reiki and meditation to the Emotional Freedom Technique (EFT), which employs tapping on certain areas or meridians to change the nervous system's response. Acupuncture, which involves the insertion of needles at strategic points in the body, can relieve osteoarthritis symptoms, in addition to chronic headache, shoulder, neck and back aches.

All of these alternative practices have been shown to alleviate stress, reduce pain and enhance a person's ability to enjoy life, but only *if* the patient uses these options regularly, and *believes* they can work. Bear in mind that positive outcomes may depend on the nature and level of the illness, as well as the person's prior experience with specifically non-medical methods.

Medical Marijuana

Though controversial, medical cannabis has been gaining ground as a valid pain therapy for adults. Research indicates that the substance can soothe severe pain, alleviate nausea and vomiting, increase appetite, reduce tremors and seizures and ease insomnia where other common medications fail. Cannabis apparently affects the *emotional* reaction to pain, but in a highly variable way. It makes pain bearable (a pain "distracter," so to speak), but does not actually decrease its intensity.

For those of us who have lived through the 1960s and 1970s, marijuana was considered a romantic expression of youthful rebellion, even a rite of passage for adolescents. Few thought about its long-term effects, especially the side effects of THC, the psychoactive ingredient in cannabis, and its addictive qualities. One in ten people who ever try marijuana will become dependent on it. The psychiatric handbook, *Diagnostic and Statistical Manual, V* of the American Psychiatric Association states that marijuana use among children 10 to 17 is correlated with a high risk of psychosis and attention-deficit disorder. The highly negative impact of marijuana on developing brains has led scientists to warn about irreversible damage to children and adolescents with even short-term use.

Nor is it a completely benign drug for adults. Although less addictive than cocaine, alcohol or nicotine, withdrawal remains a major reason why many users find marijuana hard to quit. Characteristic withdrawal symptoms from the substance run the gamut from insomnia, cravings, restlessness, loss of appetite, difficulty concentrating, sweating and mood swings to depression, irritability and anger. Drug tolerance is also an issue for long-term users. Over time, tolerance contributes to a markedly diminished effect on the user with the same amount of the substance. In other words, despite using relatively high amounts of marijuana, the user may not be able to achieve the desired effects of pain relief. Social, occupational and recreational activities may be abandoned because of efforts to obtain and pay for the substance.

Certainly, a major neurological downside of the medical use of marijuana is the drug's ill effects on working memory, contributing to forgetfulness and mental lapses associated with use. Slower reaction time weighs in as another side effect, especially dangerous for operating machinery or driving a car. The drug may also act to reduce motivation, a significant issue for younger persons and non-medical users. Serious respiratory and cardiovascular problems are associated with years of smoking marijuana. Newer, safer delivery methods have been proposed, such as using a vaporizer or oral tablets, which contain only its active ingredients.

On balance, marijuana simply cannot be deemed a magic bullet to ease symptoms of chronic pain—especially since patients may require years of continuous use.

When All Else Fails

Fentanyl transdermal patches (trade name: Duragesic) are available for "breakthrough" (or intense, unrelenting) pain that cannot be treated with standard medications. The patch is a highly effective, synthetic pain reliever that releases into body fats, and then slowly delivers the drug into the bloodstream over a 48-to-72-hour period. Fentanyl is approximately 100 times more potent than morphine and is most often used in operating rooms, intensive care units or situations where pain cannot be relieved by other means (for example, severe back pain, bone injuries, neuropathy, arthritis and cancer). Dosage depends on pain level, which can be adjusted by the size of the patch. Approximately 10 percent of patients experience major side effects, including diarrhea, nausea, constipation and headache.

Any drug has the potential for abuse. Misuse of this painkiller (for instance, changing the patch too often) has resulted in a significant number of dangerous reactions and deaths. Yet, the figure remains only one quarter the number associated with mortality from other drugs, such as methadone or hydrocodone. Signs of overdose with the patch include sudden respiratory depression, extreme fatigue and feelings of faintness or dizziness. Caregivers should be especially cautioned that their loved ones must avoid alcoholic beverages or excessive heat in the area of the patch (sauna, hot tub, electric blanket), both of which increase the impact of the medication. The best advice when using this drug? Be on the alert for improper use and stay in close contact with your prescribing physician.

*P*alliative Care – Caregivers are often at a loss when attempting to support their loved one through periods of pain and deep discomfort. Many have discovered that chronic illness requires symptom and pain management that goes beyond their regular doctor's visits or at-home remedies. Palliative care steps in with symptom management, a primary goal that focuses on relieving pain, shortness of breath, nausea, vomiting, constipation, fatigue, loss of appetite and difficulty sleeping, all of which often accompany disease or treatments to cure the disease.

Palliative care, which entails both comfort care and curing care, is provided by a team of professionals that may include physicians, nurses, social workers, chaplains, pharmacists and dietitians. They serve as a response team depending on the needs of the patient and their family. Palliative care does not replace you, the caregiver, or your physician, but works with you, your family and primary physician to support and guide the course of treatment.

You can benefit from palliative care if your loved one has been diagnosed with a complex, serious illness and needs relief from pain or symptoms. Palliative care can also be helpful if you need to make difficult decisions about how to proceed with care and treatment and need the extra professional help. I especially recommend palliative care for those who suffer from dementia and need assistance with communication issues related to their care and treatment.

Palliative care may be provided in a variety of health care settings, such as hospitals, skilled nursing facilities, hospices, assisted living or out-patient clinics. Local conditions determine where your palliative care can be found. The goal of palliative care is to improve the quality of a seriously ill person's life at whatever stage of treatment or wherever they may be located in the community.

Rather than feeling alone, helpless, confused, unprepared, tired or unable to provide for the needs of your family member or friend, you *can* reach out for support. Palliative care has served over one million patients and their families over a thirty-year period. When you turn to palliative care, you can sit back, take a breath and be reassured your loved one is in excellent hands.

Q

*Q*uestions and Answers For Your Doctor – Times
have changed. Caregivers and their elderly
charges can no longer depend upon the intimate environment of the old-fashioned doctor's style—the home
visits, the doctor's wife bringing over cookies or calling
you at home about your vitamins and diet, even bringing over a used bassinet—experiences I cherish from my
first pregnancy. So, how can caregivers deal with this
new reality of a precarious, bewildering, often indifferent medical system?

The first order of business is to learn how to talk to
your doctor. Our culture has set doctors on a pedestal,
assuming them to have godlike objectivity, wisdom and
emotional intelligence. Of course, they end up disap-
pointing us. Physicians can provide knowledge of a particular sort—they are, after all, highly trained for carrying out *specific* medical or surgical tasks. However, we
need to line up our expectations with reality.

As a caregiver, your issue is not to focus on medical
details, but to deal with you and your family's crushing
fears about your loved one's life. Atul Gawande writes

in *The New Yorker*: "A large part of the [doctor's] task is helping people negotiate the overwhelming anxiety—anxiety about death, anxiety about suffering, anxiety about loved ones, anxiety about finances…There are many worries and real terrors." Gawande recommends that all of us need to arrive at an acceptance of our own mortality, and a clear understanding of the limits and possibilities of medicine. This process may take weeks, and is rarely accomplished in a single conversation with your physician.

As a start, we can reduce the agony of the medical encounter and feel more empowered as a caregiver if we plan ahead with our questions, as well as be prepared for providing information. I invite you to try some of the following suggestions.

Bring your list of inquiries. What can we expect? Pain? How much? Where? Disability? Temporary or long-term? Mental health or behavior issues—mild, moderate or severe? If the doctor is less than forthcoming, ask the nurse or physician's assistant. Sometimes, you'll go away empty handed, but be persistent. It never hurts to ask—but we need to ask the right questions. You will have little luck inquiring about your loved one's general "prognosis" and much better results when you ask for specifics: "Is my loved one likely to be in a wheelchair six months from now?" And even—"Is my husband dying? How long will he live?"

Be informed. Ask the doctor or attending nurse to provide more detailed information about the disease that threatens your loved one's life and sanity. Go to the Web and seek out resources intended for the general public. You might also find helpful some organizations, such as Alzheimer's Association, with monthly newsletters entirely relevant for answering at least some of your questions. Your local pharmacist provides a good source of information about side effects of prescription and drug interaction effects. Don't forget your caregiver support groups. Other caregivers may be an outstanding resource both for information and support (See also Information Overload).

Be in charge of your emotions. Don't overload the doctor with your grievances. He's not likely to have the tools to comfort you. He may even look for ways to avoid you. Use your voice—as we say to our four-year olds. I predict the doctor's response will be a great deal more positive when he isn't required to read your mind or try to console you.

Expect medical miracles. We are now the beneficiaries of major advances of the past fifty years, which include antibiotics, anti-inflammatories, sophisticated non-invasive diagnostic capabilities, minimally invasive surgical techniques, immunization against a wide variety of diseases, kidney dialysis, open-heart surgery and organ transplantation. That's just a short list of medical triumphs that may renew your loved one, and hopefully, restore the person to active living.

Don't expect miracles with terminal illness. We want so much to believe that this terrible disease will go away. The doctor will pull a magic rabbit out of the hat—an astonishing drug that will completely revive our mother. The medical team will pounce upon an extraordinary (and of course, painless) surgery to restore your husband. The radiologist read the MRI wrong. Your father doesn't have brain tumors after all. Such fantasizing wastes too much time and energy. Stay in the real world of limitations and only too often, bad news.

Express an attitude of gratitude. Gratitude works wonders for overworked professional staff. Acknowledging personal services with a smile and "thank you" can smooth the edges of a long, ragged day for everyone. Eye contact with your physician, nurse or receptionist raises the human quotient of the medical encounter 100 percent. Being kind to beleaguered staff can make their day. The best part is not simply getting a more positive response, but how it makes you feel—more in charge and a more effective communicator for your loved one.

Recognize that the problem between you and the doctor could be a basic misunderstanding when confronting terminal illness. For doctors, the main point of a discussion about terminal illness is to determine what people want—whether they want chemo or not, whether they want to be resuscitated or not, whether they want Hospice or not. Their focus is to present the facts and figures that will help you—and if your loved one is cogent—make the right decision.

Develop a trusting relationship with your primary physician. If you don't have a doctor you can trust, find one, preferably before your loved one deteriorates further. You may be harboring complaints about doctors from your past. "They let Granny die without painkillers." "The damn doctor was wrong with my diagnosis, so what's the point?" This antagonistic attitude will net you little satisfaction when you attempt to seek medical assistance for your loved one. Once you've established a doctor-patient relationship you can count on, raise the following question. *Doctor—What would you do if your mother or father had terminal cancer—order more chemotherapy? Or for late stage heart failure—endure another surgery? Or silenced in the grip of a diabetic coma—demand resuscitation?* I am certain your doctor will be truthful and direct with you in your efforts to do the right thing—which is essentially what your loved one wants at the end of life.

$\mathcal{R}$

$\mathcal{R}$espite Care – Full-time, 24/7 care of your loved one is virtually impossible. Few have the motivation or energy to carry it out. Nor should you. But you'd be surprised. Many caregivers believe they can do it alone—never taking breaks and never breaking down. You learn, often too late, you have overestimated your own capacity for care. In the meantime, both you and your loved one suffer the consequences, with you feeling burned out, isolated or overwhelmed. The challenge of caregiving is to give heartfelt care while finding ways to reduce stress, restore energy and promote balance in your life. That's where a little relief comes in.

Respite care is short-term care used as a temporary alternative to your usual care arrangement. It's critical that caregivers have *regular breaks*—a trip to the grocery store, a day with friends, a weekend with your beloved daughter, a vacation to a sunny place in the midst of wintry gloom. You set the pace by learning how much time you need to recharge your batteries—and how often you need to have the pause that refreshes. Just anticipating regular relief can be a lifesaver.

Avoiding distress to your loved one is equally important. Establish early in the relationship that you will need time off. When the time comes, talk about a "little holiday" and be positive in your explanation. Any uncertainty on your part may alarm your loved one, so be calm, firm and give information in a clear and simple manner. Above all, reassure your loved one that they will be well cared for and that you will be coming home again soon. Keep in mind you are not letting your loved one down. You are lifting both of you into a more doable caregiving-care receiving relationship. Because stress is infectious, frequent timeouts will both lessen the strain, and make you a more effective caregiver.

Support is just around the corner. Try a number of approaches before you decide who the respite person or organization will be to ensure you've found a good fit for you and your loved one. Contact a family member or friend, local volunteer group, adult day health program, residential care facility or home care agency for referrals. You can even trade services with other caregivers. You'll also find caregiver support groups provide a welcome respite for you, with friendly folks who share your concerns. You can talk, vent, laugh and exchange tips with people who understand.

Funding sources may also be available, including long-term care insurance, family sources, Administration on Aging, Veteran's Administration and Social Security for patients with disability coverage. Open your heart to create a team of helpers who can bring in new energy and ideas to lighten your load and give you the boost you need to carry you through.

ex and Dementia – Sexuality among persons with dementia has become an emotionally charged issue, as millions of Boomers move into the ranks of the elderly. Geriatric specialists deem it to be normal, natural and legal if the activity is consensual or with a spouse or partner. The belief is that all adults, regardless of their mental condition, have human needs and legal rights to express themselves in a sexual manner, as long as they do not injure themselves or another person. Others question whether those rights disappear when a person has been diagnosed with dementia.

What's at stake in this contentious issue? One school claims that persons with certain kinds of dementia, such as Alzheimer's, advanced vascular dementia or late-stage Parkinson's disease, may not have the ability to consent to sex with non-intimate others. Lack of mental competence and confusion open the door to social control, they insist, with caregivers carefully monitoring any "suspicious" interactions, especially among strangers in skilled nursing facilities.

Another school of thought proposes that, although

the dementia patient has lost mental connections with people they've loved, and with much of their past, that should not rob them of their desire and need for intimacy. These are people who have become, to some degree, somebody else. Just because they're confused about whom they're with, that doesn't mean they can't receive pleasure at a time in their lives when pleasure is so rare.

Family members tend to take the first position. Who wants to think about their elderly mother having a sexual relationship with someone the family doesn't know. How do we know the man wasn't aggressive? Why would Mother do that, anyway, since her husband continues to love and care for her, regardless of her condition? Such questions and others came to light recently during a highly publicized court case.

The lawsuit in Coralville, Iowa centered around a 120-bed skilled nursing facility called Windmill Manor. Two patients, both with dementia, were found having sex. The man was 78, the woman, 87. When the woman's family inadvertently discovered their mother's sexual involvement, inasmuch as she was currently married to their father, they brought charges, accusing Windmill Manor of neglect and abuse.

Three and a half years of litigation resulted in the discharge of the administrator of the facility and his female head of nursing, and well as the termination of other staff members. The male patient involved was forced to relocate, but the only available skilled nursing facility was hours away from his family. And, the night the nurses intervened and removed the man, the woman responded by kicking, screaming and biting the nurses, expressly demonstrating her displeasure.

Nor did the evidence point to abuse; no evidence of injury or force was found. Perhaps the greatest irony is that many of the staff got their licenses back after further examination of the case.

Tempest in a teapot? Apparently not. AARP says: "It's a delicate subject and the zone is completely gray." No blanket policy on sex within old age facilities exists, especially with Alzheimer's patients. Some facilities treat the sexual relationship on a case-by-case basis. For example, does it seem consensual? Are both people single? Do the families mind? Do the sexual partners appear to be happy and comfortable as opposed to acting agitated or emotionally distraught?

The Hebrew Home at Riverdale, New York, may have set a precedent when it adopted a policy stating that "residents have the right to seek out and engage in sexual expression." Facility personnel regard sexuality as an inalienable right and assert that intimacy is good for their patients, whether or not their children approve. As long as the relationship appears consensual, and stays consensual, the policy is clear: "It is the function and responsibility of staff to uphold and facilitate sexual expression." The Hebrew Home even provides sexually explicit materials and patient privacy.

Another landmark situation involves former Supreme Court Justice Sandra Day O'Connor. After her husband developed dementia and was placed in a skilled nursing facility, he became intimate with another woman in the facility. Justice O'Connor decided that this relationship was in his best interest. She definitely wanted her husband to be as happy as possible, even with his cognitive loss. Every case is different, of course, as we know.

Addressing sexual freedom means more than simple policy changes, however. It requires staff and family to uphold and support the sexual rights of the patient, and to be objective and respectful rather than subjective and judgmental. Pepper Schwartz, a prominent sexologist, contends: "I would want this for my spouse if he had dementia, was in a care facility, and no longer remembered me." She further argues: "If you want to be sexual while you are still alive—but not quite yourself—you'd better make [written] plans to preserve your rights ahead of time."

If you are concerned that your loved one will be engaged in potentially unsafe intimate behavior when in care, you need to discuss this with facility staff *before* it becomes an issue.

*S*ubstance Abuse – *"I don't remember my Dad ever drinking this much. The neighbor lady called me today and told me in strictest confidence 'the garbage can was loaded with beer and gin bottles.'"*

Although family members and friends are often reluctant to disclose their elderly loved one's substance abuse or mental health issues, addiction is no longer a family's well-kept secret. *The New York Times* reports that we are in the midst of an epidemic of elderly drug and alcohol abuse and mental illness that has yet to be recognized. An estimated 14 to 20 percent of the population 65 and older has a substance abuse or mental health problem.

The New York Times recently reported:

> *Detecting drug or alcohol problems in the elderly is difficult in part because family members and clinicians are reluctant to ask about it. Perhaps it's just a form of ageism, but drug abuse is not the first thing that pops into the mind of physicians when they encounter an older patient.*

Statistics further clarify the extent of the issue:

- 2.5 million older adults have an alcohol or drug problem.
- Six to 11 percent of elderly hospital admissions, 14 percent of older adults emergency room admissions and 20 percent of senior psychiatric hospital admissions are the direct result of alcohol or drug problems.
- Widowers over the age of 75 have the highest rate of alcoholism in the United States.
- Nearly 50 percent of nursing home residents have had alcohol-related problems, which ultimately resulted in their incapacitation.
- Older adults are hospitalized as often for alcohol-related problems as for heart attacks.
- Almost 17 million prescriptions for tranquilizers are prescribed for older Americans each year.

- Benzodiazepines, a type of sedative, are the most commonly misused and abused prescription medications.

Even when doctors make a connection between substance use/abuse and medical or psychiatric problems, they may fail to recognize that even modest amounts of alcohol or drugs can be problematic. Older patients have a significantly reduced ability to metabolize these substances, as well as increased sensitivity to their mental effects. Doctors can also mistake addiction symptoms, such as rapid heartbeat, forgetfulness or frequent falling, with normal issues of aging.

A number of other factors contribute to substance abuse, which includes alcohol, psychoactive drugs and recreational use of prescription drugs. Elders may be self-medicating to deal with grief over the loss of a spouse or friend. Or they may have mild cognitive impairment (see entry), making it difficult to self-monitor their usage. The elderly rarely turn to substances to "get high," but instead to alleviate the physical and psychological pain from medical and psychiatric illness. Social isolation also drives an elderly person into addiction.

Rather than caregivers sitting helplessly by when they clearly suspect an addiction problem, they can, as a caring person, intervene. Experts tell us that caregivers should proceed without judgment or rancor. *The Working Caregiver's* advice is "to proactively sit down with the older adult suspected of alcohol or drug abuse to assess the current situation." Treatment is often the only recourse for elders who refuse to seek help for abusive alcohol or drug behavior.

Expect the addict to resist, be defensive, make excuses, and tell you "it's not your problem." These are cover-ups often associated with problem drinking and drug use. Consulting a professional could facilitate a more rapid recovery. Common symptoms range from slurred speech, decreased appetite, irritability and mood instability to weight loss, insomnia and blackouts. Be on the alert for social withdrawal, depression, anxiety or a break with reality, as well as hiding or denying use of alcohol or drugs. Remember: no situation is too out of control to warrant help and intervention.

*S*undowner's Syndrome – As an Alzheimer or dementia caregiver you may have noticed that in the late afternoon or early evening your loved one experiences increased fear, anger, outbursts, agitation and other behavior changes. Not all patients who suffer from dementia or Alzheimer's disease exhibit what is termed "sundowner's" symptoms. Some patients exhibit symptoms of dementia all day, which grow worse in the late afternoon and evening, while others may exhibit no symptoms at all until the sun goes down.

Sundowner's syndrome largely remains a mystery to medical science, although there are several theories about why these symptoms begin at twilight. Research has focused on determining the exact cause, but studies show a variety of origins. One idea is that it's an accumulation of all of the sensory stimulation from the day, which can overwhelm and cause stress. Other studies propose that it's caused by hormonal imbalances that occur mainly at night. Two other notions conclude that "sundowning" is a result of simple fatigue, or it may be anxiety caused by the inability to see as well in the dark. Almost all of the research concludes that a state of confusion at the end of the day is directly related to: fatigue, low lighting, increased shadows, and disruption of the body's internal clock.

The theory that the symptoms have something to do with darkness has been supported by studies where the symptoms subside within an hour of the return of daylight. Evidence also suggests that nursing facility patients show an increase in sundowner's symptoms during winter, which may point to a correlation with seasonal affective disorder (SAD). SAD is believed to cause depression in winter because of shorter periods of sunlight, which can affect people of all ages.

Several factors may increase the risk for sundowning among those with dementia. Pain, infection or severe constipation are leading contenders that contribute to agitation. Poor nourishment and excessive medication can readily shift the dementia patient into confusion and anxiety. A noisy or disruptive sleeping environment, characteristic of some long-term care facilities, can prevent proper sleep, leaving mind and body in an exhausted state.

Symptoms and Prevention

Symptoms typically associated with sundowning range from pacing, rocking, fear and restlessness to agitation and anger. Crying spells and low mood are not uncommon. Caregivers are sometimes alarmed at their loved one's "shadowing" behavior, which involves following them closely wherever they go. More difficult symptoms include paranoia, wandering, violence, hallucinations and hiding things. Whatever the causes of sundowning, the result is always stressful and troubling for both patient and caregiver.

Once you focus on ways to make sundown syndrome less severe, caregivers can move forward with solutions. Here are a few approaches to reduce the most extreme symptoms:

Activity. Being more active during the day may help dementia patients sleep better at night.
- Discourage long daytime naps.
- Encourage exercise, like walking.
- Foster hobbies that get dementia patients up and moving.

Healthy Diet. Caregivers should make sure their loved one gets the proper nourishment and fluids.
- Limit caffeine and sugar to the morning hours.
- Plan an early dinner.
- Keep snacks light before bedtime.

Bedtime. Creating a soothing environment for sleep can diminish anxiety and lessen more severe symptoms.

- Allow the patient to change bedrooms or sleep in a favorite chair or couch.

- Introduce restful music or nature sounds.

- Set up a calming routine, such as a story or backrub, at least a half hour before bedtime.

- Keep a night light on to reduce agitation when surroundings are dark or unfamiliar.

Medical intervention. Ask the doctor to look for physical problems, such as pain, infection or bladder problems that may contribute to nighttime confusion and agitation.

- Be on the lookout for physical sources of disturbing behavior, especially in late-stage dementia.

- Review prescription medications to make sure they are still needed.

- Check with a specialist to see if supplements, such as melatonin or other remedies, could minimize the disorientation associated with sundowning.

- In unfamiliar settings, such as a hospital, bring comforting items, such as photos, radio or CD player from home.

When sundowning occurs in a care facility, it may be related to the increased bustle of activity during shift changes. Staff transitions can upset residents, particularly if they result in gaps in service. In some institutions dinner, toileting and bedtime preparations may collide with staff dinners or breaks, conditions that invariably disrupt the schedule. You might consider visiting your loved one during this time and observing the facility's routines to identify any ongoing issues.

*T*eamwork – We all know what a team is—a group of people who pull together for a common cause. Teamwork depends upon *everyone* pooling their efforts and energies to produce a single outcome. An effective team can outdo by far any single individual effort, regardless of how brilliant or talented that individual may be.

Corporations depend upon teamwork. In fact, they seek employees who can demonstrate they can be a "collaborative team builder." Lone wolves need not apply.

Why is it that people continue to operate under the illusion that one caregiver can do it all? "Mary can do it. She just rolls up her sleeves and gets 'er done." This expectation usually applies to a wife, daughter, daughter-in-law or even granddaughter, who are all expected to have some hidden gift for taking care of an ill loved one. When the designated caregiver collapses under the weight of an impossible job, fingers get pointed and judgments are made. She becomes "less than," a failure at what she *should* naturally be doing.

We need an updated model for family caregiving. Let's

try the "collaborative team builder" approach on for size. How would it look? How could it serve to spread around the responsibility and the satisfaction of caregiving to a number of family members?

- You begin with the decision maker, the family CEO, as it were. Every family has one. Let that person take charge of major decisions, such as legal, medical, institutional placement, and others.

- At the same time, every decision must be made collaboratively. No surprises. Keep the family informed and get their input using phone calls, social media or e-mail. Never allow a single person to make an irrevocable choice without consulting everyone.

- Scout out other family members and figure out what talents or resources they can bring to the table. Be cautious about assignments. Simply because your brother is an accountant doesn't necessarily mean he should take over dad's financial matters.

- Many caregivers confront the situation of the non-cooperative relative. Bob refuses to visit his loved one, provide respite time or even talk on the phone. He simply doesn't want to deal with it. As unbelievable as this seems, it's fairly common. Why not request this family member to contribute financially? Every family knows what needs to be done to loosen the deep pockets of the absent member.

- The hands-on caregiver is actually in the best position to serve as the CEO—coordinating tasks and connecting the dots. To keep the system going, the CEO can keep everyone informed on a regular basis. Complete the role by adding two more components: *motivate* and *encourage* family members to continue relating to their loved one. Their love and attention needs to go beyond a medical crisis to participate in the long term.

Don't forget. To be an effective CEO, you'll need to *make* time to take care of yourself. You are the most critical player in this dynamic. Your good health, strength and courage will ensure the best outcomes for both you and your loved one.

U

Uncertainty – Modern medicine has such a vault-ed reputation for healing that we invariably an-ticipate a full recovery, even when we've been seriously ill. Cancer is a case in point. In former years, a cancer diagnosis was a death sentence—it was only a matter of time. A similar outcome occurred with heart disease and other chronic ailments. Now, we address illness in terms of *type* of disease, general *health* of the patient, *stages* or *levels*, *treatment* protocol (which often must be tailored to the individual) and the possibility of *remission* and *recovery*. Risk analysis further pinpoints the likelihood whether a person will survive a particular medical prob-lem, or succumb to it.

Yet, no matter how much precision science can bring to bear on an illness, the situation for any one person is never totally certain. Outcomes depend on many factors: the patient's genetics, environment, social support, per-sonal habits and preferences, coping skills and even per-sonality. You may know a particular disease has a typi-cal trajectory—the course of that disease over time—but how it tracks for any specific individual can be wholly unpredictable. And in many situations, you must play a waiting game before your loved one is diagnosed or treated.

Arthur Roeser, author of *Notes from a Problem Child*, writes about a family's fear and anxiety as they wait in the hospital for the sluggish medical system to tell them what happened to their beloved husband and father after his stroke. The son turns to his mother.

> *"We hugged her, but she was limp—wrung out like a spent washcloth. 'Mom, what's going on? What did they say is wrong?' She didn't know. Nurses had told her that they'd have to wait until the hospital wing doctor saw him and that wouldn't be until the morning. They'd have to wait and see until a neurologist saw him. They'd have to wait until one of the doctors ordered tests; an x-ray, an MRI, a [CT] scan, before they could ascertain what it was or how to proceed, before they could prescribe anything. They'd have to wait until the speech therapist evaluated whether or not he could swallow and therefore, eat or drink or take medicine orally. The last thing he had eaten was a turkey sandwich at home a couple of days ago."*

So, how can you cope with the uncertainty that surrounds your loved one's situation?

1. Accept the fact that you have no control either over the disease, your loved one's response to the

disease or circumstances surrounding medical intervention.

2. Recognize that change is inevitable—and often not to your liking. The issue resides in your *reaction* to change.

3. Understand that despite all the research you may have unearthed in your effort to comprehend the parameters of your loved one's illness, unknown or incalculable conditions can alter a hopeful outcome. For instance, the survival rate for heart attacks has increased immensely. Exercise, healthy food, good social support and a positive attitude can recharge the patient—in some cases, she may be healthier than ever after recovery. But if the heart patient also has diabetes or other chronic disease, or fails to follow the post-heart attack regimen, the scenario can be very different. You may be looking at an extended period of decline and debilitation.

4. Avoid taking on the role of the expert on your loved one's disease to family and friends. You may have abundant information about an illness, but keep in mind that every patient behaves in his or her own unique way. Medicine is an inexact science at best, regardless of how advanced it seems to the lay person.

5. Once a diagnosis and treatment plan has been outlined, rise to the challenge by motivating your loved one to follow the new regime. For instance,

diabetes is now one of the most common diseases that family physicians and internists treat. A patient may come into the doctor's office with typical symptoms—parched with thirst, eating and drinking excessively, losing weight, blurry eyes and exhaustion—without either patient or caregiver having a clue as to the cause. Dr. Danielle Ofri, Associate Professor of Medicine at New York University School of Medicine, says: "A new diagnosis of diabetes is an enormous undertaking, much to explain, major life changes to contemplate, myths to dispel, consultations with a nutritionist and a diabetes nurse." The caregiver's primary task will be to stay the course as the patient adjusts to the radical departure in lifestyle.

6. The most productive way to deal with uncertainty and to gain a greater sense of ease is to put aside your expectations. Rather than worry about why, what, when or how your loved one's prospects may turn out, stay in the NOW. Be optimistic, but temper positivity with the reality of your loved one's physical and mental condition. Once you can overcome the temptation to engage in wishful thinking, you are on your way to being a well-balanced caregiver.

V

eterans' Special Needs – As our wounded warriors come home from the longest period of war in American history, Americans have given little attention to the injured veterans of Iraq and Afghanistan, in terms of the family members who must look after them. This is a significantly different returning veteran than one from World War II, Korea or Vietnam, to say the least.

The New York Times reports that more than half a million soldiers have suffered from brain-rattling concussions of the approximately 2.34 million U.S. personnel deployed since the start of military operations in 2001. One result is an epidemic of Combat Occupation Stress Disorder, Traumatic Brain Injury (TBI) and Post Traumatic Stress Disorder (PTSD).

In the post-9/11 era, service members survive their wounds in considerably higher numbers than previous wars because of advancements in body armor, helmets and improved battlefield medical treatment. Currently, the survival rate for wounded soldiers is about 90 percent, due to timely and effective application of emergency medical care.

The enemy's use of the improvised explosive device (IED) has more insidious and devastating effects than more traditional battlefield weapons in terms of the extensive and excruciating wounds produced. Such devices have resulted in multiple amputations, horrendous burns, TBI, spinal cord injuries and blindness. Spinal cord injuries, moreover, have been linked with cardiovascular disease, especially in later life. Multiple injuries, internal organ damages and chronic pain, suffered by a large number of returning soldiers, are often very difficult to treat. Whether the wounds are physical, cognitive, psychological or psychosocial, many veterans face a grueling rehabilitation process.

TBI is the "signature injury" resulting from these wars. Extended deployments have also led to *permanent* physical and mental disability, as well as high rates of suicide among returning soldiers. Unlike physical injuries, mental disabilities often show up months after release from the service, throwing the burden smack at unprepared and resource-limited families.

Military caregivers, so-called by the Veterans Administration (VA), are the estimated 275,000 to more than one million wives, mothers, children, friends and other family members who serve their disabled loved ones. Caregiving for this new crop of veterans presents distinct challenges as care receivers may be stronger and more dangerous, unlike elderly or non-veteran family members.

Veterans suffering from TBI and other combat-related brain injuries may not show outward signs of disability, but have severe problems with memory, mood, concentration, headaches, dizziness, loss of balance and sleep. Caregivers often must be on guard for outbursts of anger, withdrawal, depression, paranoia and other typical symptoms of PTSD, which accompanies TBI.

Even mild TBI contributes to a round-the-clock caregiving schedule, including such basic activities as bathing, dressing, eating, using the toilet, making medical appointments, managing finances or struggling through emotional difficulties. Friendships, household tasks and even child care take second place after caring for the disabled person. Confronting the maze of government agencies, health insurance, medical providers and community services can be the most daunting task of all.

The face of the new "war widow" is surprisingly young, and bearing a tremendous load of caring for a younger-aged spouse who is still alive, but requires constant care and attention. She is also likely to be raising young children. In one heart-wrenching story, a small boy of seven said to his mother, "Mom, all my friends' daddies are grown up. When will my daddy grow up?"

"Veteran Voices," a blog by Ken Olsen, offers stories of the upside-down lives of spouses and parents of severely injured veterans.

> *"PTSD sufferers are like toddlers, teenagers and grumpy old men all in one," says one caregiver. "The blast changed the fabric of our family," says another. "I couldn't breathe without him tearing me down," whispered an overwrought wife.*

"High intensity" caregiving, that is, providing care for more than 80 hours a week, is particularly common for veterans with TBI. Mentally incapacitated veterans have often been compared to late-stage Alzheimer disease patients: constantly confused, disoriented and helpless. Implicit pressure from government agencies and physicians, and a lack of options tend to prevent these overburdened wives from abandoning their disabled husbands.

Families and local friends are often of little comfort. They may even question the facts of their relative's disability—or worse—blame the victim. "What's the matter with him?" "Why isn't he going to work?" "What are you doing to him that keeps him from hanging out with us?" And even crueler: "He's been a complete wreck since he married you."

Families of veterans from other wars are especially critical of their loved one's incapacitation, and compare it unfavorably with their own "pull yourselves up by your bootstraps" post-war experiences. Caregivers are often forced to pack up and move their families away from these harmful influences. Isolated and exhausted, military wife caregivers can look forward to a lifetime of this unending obligation.

Often regularly employed workers before their husband returned, military wives caring for their disabled loved one face an overwhelming task: full-time caregiver, full-time parent and full-time worker. Unable to leave their loved one, caregivers may attempt to shuffle their work schedule, reduce hours or take temporary leave. In time, many surrender to the inevitability that they can't do it all, and sacrifice promotions, health insurance and retirement benefits to stay home. The physical and emotional toll can be substantial. Depleted resources and loneliness add to the bleakness of the caregiver's life.

Although the cornerstone of support for our nation's wounded, ill and injured veterans, military caregivers have largely been abandoned to their fate. The nearly total absence of a national strategy for veterans' caregivers has not gone unnoticed, however. The Elizabeth Dole Foundation commissioned the RAND Corporation to assess the needs of military caregivers, scan the services available to them and identity how their needs are—and are not—being met.

The RAND Report concluded that the needs of returning wounded warriors have recently been the subject of significant inquiry and national policy concerns, as well as the focus of much private philanthropy. "But the needs of their caregivers remain largely overlooked." Despite saving the government millions of dollars, deferring or delaying institutionalization, and thus reducing medical costs, the home remains a shadow environment. Their key findings conclude that military caregivers:

- Are a unique caregiver population because of their youth and having dependent-aged children.

- Experience special challenges, because they also act as case managers navigating complex health systems, advocating for new treatment and serving as financial and legal representatives for their loved one.

- Suffer disproportionately from physical and mental health problems and emotional distress.
- Have limited help because many government programs are in their infancy and community resources are scattered and uncoordinated. Lack of access appears to be a major hindrance preventing military caregivers from receiving assistance or benefits.

Rather than abandoning these women to continue to toil in "relative obscurity," the Elizabeth Dole Foundation provided grants to several organizations in 2011. The National Military Family Association develops caregiver best practices, while the Military Officers' Association of America focuses on legal and financial planning assistance to these families. The Military Child Education Coalition's mission is specifically to address the needs of children affected by their parent's injuries.

Services for family caregivers of post-9/11 veterans are slowly moving into place. The United States Department of Veterans Affairs now accepts applications under the *Caregivers and Veterans Omnibus Health Services Act of 2010*. This legislation offers comprehensive services for eligible veterans. Among the proposed support for primary family caregivers:

- *Monthly stipend* for personal care services averaging $1200 to $2400 a month (not aimed to match job wages, but to assist with personal care).
- *Travel expenses* include lodging and per diem while accompanying veterans undergoing care.

- *Access to health insurance* if the caregiver is not already entitled to care or services under a health care plan.
- *Mental health services and counseling.*
- *Comprehensive VA Caregiver Training* provided by Easter Seals.
- *Respite care* (not less than 30 days per year).

If you are one of those post-9/11 eligible military families that qualify for this support, or know someone who is, check with your local VA. Caregiver Support Coordinators have been set up at every VA Medical Center to assist veterans and their family caregivers with the application process. Be prepared, though, for a tortuously slow move through the outdated claims system. As one 3-75th Ranger veteran commented:

> *Disgraceful is an understatement. Many vets that I have talked to drop their claim because of all the hassle. It is like the VA operates against the vet, and tries to discourage vets from getting any kind of help.*

While veterans wait for their claims to be processed so that they can cover health care expenses, many see their medical conditions worsen. Nearly 20,000 veterans have died while waiting for their disability claims to be processed, leading Ned Resnikoff to describe the system as a "national disgrace." The VA has committed to eliminate the backlog by 2015, but switching from the antiquated paper filing system to processing the claims electronically isn't so easy. It may still take months or even years for many veterans' families to receive benefits. The VA is no longer the only resource, though.

The Department of Defense offers programs for affected families, such as Military One Source, which has trained counselors, staffed 24 hours a day. A host of private organizations have also cropped up to help fill in the gaps. For example, Lotsa Helping Hands coordinates assistance via an online community of more than 1 million volunteers and fellow caregivers. Injured veterans can also register for a variety of family support services at The Wounded Warrior Project. After years of neglect, military family caregivers can reach out for help and support—and hopefully find it.

Last, but never least, caring for the caregiver should be a priority for all military caregivers. It's important to take some time to unwind and recharge drained batteries. The stress and strain of looking after a disabled loved one requires that caregivers pay attention to their own needs, as well. Caregivers who nurture themselves with "time-out" periods, contact with friends and involvement in a support group will experience increased strength and renewed energy. Such interludes can also shake off that dreary self-pity that is an ever-present threat to effective, loving caregiving.

W

When Home Care Is Not Enough – Regardless of how extraordinary your caregiving skills may be, the time comes when home care can no longer be sustained. At some point, caregivers must confront their own limitations in the face of the overwhelming physical and emotional needs of the patient. Nearly 50 percent of us will be facing institutional placement at some point in our elder years, so try to be realistic and accept the need to make changes. Before things become desperate for you and your loved one, make an effort to recognize when care in the home is simply *not* working.

Let's take a look at some conditions that point the way for placement in a more secure setting. The first is obvious—when a crisis occurs and your loved one requires extensive medical treatment beyond your ability to provide it. Care in assisted living or a skilled nursing facility can be short-term, as in rehabilitation after hospitalization, or may be a permanent solution for a chronic condition.

Although most of us procrastinate about placing our loved one, institutional care can become a necessity in certain situations. For example, when your loved one has advanced dementia and may be causing harm to self or others, placement is no longer optional. As difficult as this may be to confront, many suffering from dementia cannot be kept at home. Wandering and getting lost or injured, even in once-familiar territory, is a common symptom of Alzheimer's disease, as is a loss of impulse control. Under the guidance of a trained care force, the caretaker can take a breath, knowing her loved one is safe in a controlled environment.

Yet another reason for placement arises when care shifts from daytime hours to round-the-clock. Or, say your loved one can no longer maintain his or her own activities of daily living (ADLs)—bathing, toileting, moving from bed to toilet, feeding, and other basics—even the most dedicated caregiver needs help. Many caregivers find that bringing in paid, professional caregivers for a few hours a day works—for a while. However, costs can mount quickly if you plan to maintain a critically ill loved one in the home. For example, you can pay as high as $150,000 per year for 24/7 care.

Coping with long-term care over months and years in the home ultimately gets to be too much for some caregivers, which contributes to burnout or illness. If you can locate the right facility for your loved one, you may be able to create a family care team that supports you and your loved one. You can continue with your regular visits, and as an advocate for your patient, work collaboratively with facility personnel when the need arises.

Additionally, seeking social, psychological and

financial help when placement is required can make all the difference. The first step? Contact your local Area Agency on Aging for referrals and recommendations. The next is finding other services, such as hospital-sponsored caregiver support groups, private counseling, an elder lawyer and accountant, as well as medical support specialists.

When you reach out for aid to ease your loved one out of home care, you will find the care community ready and willing to assist you during this time of transition.

*W*omen and Caregiving – Is a personal commitment to care for an elderly ailing family member limited to women? Certainly, men find themselves equally challenged to give care to their aging mother or sick wife. But in our culture women are expected to take on the caregiving duties, and are more likely to sacrifice health, careers, hopes and dreams to care for the older generation or their own aged spouse. Keep in mind, also, that when it comes to caring for older spouses, wives fare worse, physically and emotionally than husbands.

Women tend to marry men older than themselves, and men generally have more health problems and shorter lives. So, it's typically the woman taking care of the man. Research from the University of California, San Francisco shows that older women have high rates of depression, poor health and a greater need for help even before the caregiving begins. When the wife is ill, men are more likely to indicate they are "helping" their wives, rather than taking on the caregiving responsibilities.

Women's caregiving styles differ, as well. Women are far more likely to intensify their care, investing more time and being more psychologically involved, especially for spouses. Men, in general, tend to delay retirement to bolster declining family fortunes. Women are more likely to decrease work hours, or quit work altogether. Women's caregiving places a significant strain on their retirement incomes. Smaller pensions, as well as reduced Social Security amounts and other retirement payments are the consequences of both reduced hours on the job and fewer hours in the workforce.

If you are a working woman caregiver, what is the message here? Carefully consider your options before you reduce work hours or quit your job to give full-time care. Can you afford to quit? Does your loved one have resources that can be used for their care? Can you find family members or friends to help take your loved one to the doctor or handle other chores? If you are a younger generation caregiver, could you live with your parent? Or could your parent live with you?

You may find agency help, which can do many of the tasks that need to be done, without risking your own economic well-being. Single women caregivers who left jobs and friends to take over caregiving are especially prone to be both emotionally bereft and financially destitute after the caregiving journey is over. Seek support early on to avoid the depression and health problems that invariably occur if a person is overworked, stressed out or without adequate resources.

$$\mathcal{X}$$

Xenophobia – Here's maybe a new term for you, but certainly not a new idea. Xenophobia refers to the irrational fear or hatred of strangers. As a caregiver, why fear the stranger or resist the new and strange events and persons happening in your life? At some point, many caregivers become fearful of change. You resist because you are simply overwhelmed: with hospitals and rehabilitation centers, with the army of specialists who can't seem to bring relief, and with the constantly changing requirements for maintaining your loved one's life. The must-do's add up: the medications with their side effects, the diets that lack taste or texture, the professional dictates for the patient requiring your full attention.

Or when your loved one, who suffers from dementia, absolutely and categorically rejects bringing in *anyone* to assist you—even the Merry Maids for house cleaning or trained practical nurse from a home health care agency. Only *you* will do for the ever-expanding list of caregiving tasks.

Consider recognizing xenophobia for what it is—simple fear of change exaggerated to the ultimate degree. You know how contagious fear is. When your loved one hyperventilates at the thought of outside relief, you can easily feel a sense of doom.

Now is the time for that conversation with your loved one—probably long overdue. You can explain very simply that you must have help to continue caregiving. Be clear. Be brief. Be firm. Helpers are only strangers for a moment until they learn the household routine. Let them enter your sanctuary. Open the doors to change, feel the fresh air. Embrace the possibility that when you extend yourself to others without hesitation, your loved one is likely to follow your lead. If not, continue your fearless efforts to create a caregiving environment that works for you—so you can more lovingly continue giving the care you know your loved one needs.

oung Caregivers – For many children, the caregiving journey begins far too early. As many as
1.4 million children and adolescents between the ages
of eight and 18 in the United States provide care for an
older adult or sibling. Approximately 400,000 of these
youngsters are between eight and 11 years old. Mostly
invisible to social agencies, many of these children are
members of minority groups and live in single parent,
low-income homes.

What's expected of these young caregivers who take
care of ill, injured, elderly or disabled family members?
The National Alliance of Caregivers shows these children handle regular domestic duties, provide personal
care and emotional support, as well as more complex
tasks that could be challenging even for their adult
counterparts.

- One third of child caregivers help with
  medications.
- Thirty-five percent of children of minority groups
  report having no help or training in dispensing

medications, compared to 11 percent in non-minority households.

- Seventeen percent help the care recipient communicate with medical providers.
- Almost half of the caregivers report they spend "a lot of time" caregiving.

A recent story from *The New York Times* clarifies how essential these children are to family maintenance.

> *"Partly paralyzed with diabetes and colitis, Linda Lent needs extensive care at home. But with her husband working long hours as a bus driver, Mrs. Lent, 47, relies on a caregiver who travels by school bus, toting a homework-filled backpack: her 13-year-old daughter, Annmarie. [On a daily basis] Annmarie injects migraine medicine, takes blood from her mother's finger for tests, and responds to seizures—responsibilities she, at times, finds overwhelming."*

Young caregivers, who put their lives on hold, often for years, are at significantly higher risk for anxiety and depression. These children are also more likely to fall asleep in class, fall behind on assignments and drop out of school. Because kids "don't want to be singled out," they avoid telling teachers about their obligations at home. The Bill and Melinda Gates Foundation found nearly one-quarter of all dropouts in the United States leave school to care for a family member. Many continue to care for their loved ones well into adulthood.

"They're very afraid of being different. Being a caregiver is very different," said Carol Levine, Director of Families and Health Care at the United Hospital Fund. Boys in particular exhibit aggressive and antisocial tendencies. Stories can be tragic, as one former male child caregiver related in a blog:

> *"I was a child caregiver for my father who suffered from a variety of diseases and was a multiple amputee. My mother was not present.... Now I can see the toll it took on the other parts of my life. It (caregiving) separated me from friends (as most of the time when I wasn't caring for him, I was working and caring for the house). I had to drop out of college (I tried three times to make it work), because I couldn't schedule regular classes due to how often he would need to see the doctor or go in for dialysis. When he passed away, I had no support... and was suddenly homeless with no friends good enough to rely this heavily on and no near family, and now—no purpose."*

Other children describe their caregiving as having both negative and positive effects. Some say they are "a more knowledgeable, compassionate person" from the experience. Others commented that it "helped make me successful [because of] my tremendous work ethic" or they just did it themselves because they encountered "too much red tape" when they attempted to reach out. Would they do it again? One young woman, who first gave care to her mother with bone cancer until she died, then looked after her severely disabled father for over five years, all without any help from family members, sums it up:

> *"As both a child caregiver and an adult caregiver, I will say despite the emotional and physical strain, if I had to do it again I would, only with a greater voice."*

Why don't child caregivers ask for help and reach out to family, neighbors, friends and social agencies? The reason they don't speak up is simple: They're afraid they will be taken away from home. Or their beloved care receiver will be taken away from their care, and placed in a skilled nursing facility. The collapse of the extended family implies that most families live away from their relatives, so the burden falls to the child and pride can prevent them from reaching out to anyone, much less close neighbors, even if they know or trust them. Family privacy and preservation are their primary concerns.

Top 10 CNN Hero, Connie Siskowski, who works with child caregivers, recounted that "These children suffer silently behind closed doors…. They don't have the help and the support and the recognition that they need." Unfortunately, organizations that monitor child caregivers do not even see the ones who get lost, the ones who wind up in jail or on the streets because they faced too much at home.

If you, a family member, or someone you know is involved in child caregiving, take heart. While children may believe no exit strategy exists for them—after all, "there's no one else to do it"—child caregiving is receiving more public attention, especially in other countries. England and Wales, as well as Australia and Canada, are moving forward with programs to prevent a child's normal life course from being disrupted by early caregiving responsibilities.

The Canadian province of British Columbia supports young caregivers and their families with timely, responsive assistance. Young caring is viewed as a function of an under-resourced government and private system of family and adult care. While admitting that a comprehensive care system is not yet in place, support programs range from respite services and community events to online, peer-to-peer counseling and national helplines for young caregivers seeking confidential information or advice. Drawing these youngsters out of the shadows is the first order of the day.

Working together with health and caregiving organizations, this program offers a multi-tiered, "whole family" approach to supporting young people and their families. The program strives to:

1. Identify and access families to provide support to prevent youngsters from taking on parenting roles that undermine their development, and create stress and anxiety.

2. Protect children from risks to their independence, safety and welfare by providing integrated family services and emotional support.

3. Help young caregivers to achieve their potential and have the same access to education and career choices and broader opportunities as their peers.

4. Assist parents who have mental or physical illness that disrupts their parenting role.

For the United States, the time is long overdue for better recognition and greater participation of young caregivers and their families in social services and community programs. Every family and community needs to pitch in and reach out to these children who have taken on adult roles, often years before they are emotionally mature enough to manage the heavy burden.

Z

ero Tolerance for Elder Abuse, Neglect and Exploitation – Imagine yourself, an aged or severely disabled person, helpless and dependent on relatives, caregivers, neighbors or institutional staff. You will obviously need a truly trustworthy person or staff person—one who is beyond reproach—to manage your daily life, including assisting you with medicines, food, bathing, bill paying and other necessities. With whom do you have complete confidence that your basic needs and interests will be met, one that you can assume in your heart is faithful and reliable? For millions of elderly and disabled Americans, that trustworthy individual or institution simply does not exist.

Elder abuse statistics provide a glimpse into the magnitude of the problem, and reveal the extent to which this population too often falls victim to various kinds of mistreatment and untimely death. Elder abuse can happen to anyone, from all socioeconomic backgrounds, cultures, ethnicities and genders (although women are most likely to be victimized). Experts are now calling elder abuse an "epidemic." Here are some of the shocking figures for 2010 submitted by the National Center on Elder Abuse, Bureau of Justice Statistics (June, 18, 2013).

- Number of reported elder abuse cases: **5,961,568**.
- Percent of elderly population abused: **9.5%**.
- Percent of female elder abuse victims: **67.3%**.
- Median age of elder abuse victims: **77.9 years old**.
- Percent of white victims: **66.4%**.
- Percent of black victims: **18.7%**.
- Percent of Hispanic victims: **10.4%**.

Racial disparities in reporting suggest that whites are much more likely both to report mistreatment and to receive Adult Protective Services than are black or Hispanic victims. Take these reporting figures with a grain of salt, though. Most elder abuse cases never see the light of day, because of the high rate of underreporting. As an example, for every one case of self-reported elder abuse in the New York State Elder Abuse Prevalence Study, 24 cases went unreported. Vulnerable and often isolated, elderly victims have long tended to fall under the criminal justice radar.

The least trustworthy group, surprisingly, may be the elderly person's most cherished intimates: adult children and spouses, who account for 66% of all abuse cases. Even worse, 42% of all murder victims over the age of 60 are killed by their own offspring.

Older adults, who are subject to abuse, neglect and exploitation, face a three times greater risk of being hospitalized than other seniors. Experts warn that frequent admissions, especially by patients with cardiovascular disease or dementia, are often a signal that elderly persons are put in situations that threaten their health and safety.

Who is most at risk for becoming a victim of elder abuse? Based on available information, women, homebound or isolated elders, those who have dementia, mental health or substance abuse problems, lower-income persons, and individuals ages 80 and over are most likely to be victims. In addition, watch out for caregivers or family members who have mental health or substance abuse issues, as they are often the culprit.

Let's also consider more specific *warning signs* of elder abuse to better protect friends, loved ones and yourself.

Physical Abuse can be identified by inadequately explained fractures, bruises, welts, cuts, sores or burns. Unexplained sexually transmitted diseases can signal sexual exploitation by family members, neighbors or institutional staff or residents. To be on the safe side, any person with close access to a dependent elder should be monitored carefully both for physical or sexual assault.

Neglect accounts for almost 60 percent of all elder abuse cases, and has a number of clear warning signs. Look for some of the following: lack of basic hygiene or appropriate clothing, lack of food, lack of medical aids (glasses, walker, hearing aid, medications), and a person confined in bed without care, untreated bed sores or pressure ulcers.

When the person lives at home, be alert to a house

that is cluttered, dirty or in disrepair or lacks adequate facilities (non-functioning or lack of stove, refrigerator, heating or cooling, plumbing or electricity). Sudden weight loss certainly can be an indication of serious illness, but also consider whether a perpetrator has withheld money for basic necessities, such as food, heat and medications.

Self-Neglect is a controversial and unresolved issue. How do you know who may be suffering from self-neglect? Elders with various medical or social conditions, such as long-term chronic illness, physical impairment, cognitive impairment, overmedication, depression, limited financial resources and isolation may **not** be competent to care for themselves, rather than their engaging in willful self-neglect. An undiagnosed mental illness or dementia may also render an older person susceptible. Other conditions can severely impair self-care, as well. Some older adults develop substance abuse problems in their later years in response to depression, stress, loss, pain or anxiety. When individuals live on the edge financially, they may be negligent and fail to take their medication or to prepare nourishing meals, because they simply cannot afford to adequately care for themselves.

Caregiver Neglect is often overlooked in elder abuse cases. In many instances, self-neglect may cover up what is, in fact, caregiver neglect. This occurs when the person responsible for the older adult or the adult with a disability fails to provide the necessary services to maintain the individual's mental or physical health.

Benign Neglect is most common. Let's begin with

the premise that caregiving can be extremely stressful and overwhelming. Spouses, children, friends and other adult relatives may become burned out and impatient as the health of their charge deteriorates. An older spouse may lack the energy or health to care for his or her loved one. Or caregivers may simply be too busy with job, family and other responsibilities to carry out the daily care regime. Intentional neglect is a different story. An alarm should sound off, if one or more of these caregiver conditions occur.

- Problems with drugs or alcohol
- History of abuse toward others
- Anger toward the adult for whom care is being provided
- Lack of family support
- Lack of knowledge of mental/physical impairments experienced by the person for whom care is being provided
- Poor problem-solving skills
- Caretaker reluctance or the feeling of being forced to provide care.

Prevention and Intervention are proactive measures for reducing caregiver neglect. Choose your caregiver by interviewing potential caregivers carefully. To prevent isolation, call and visit periodically. Offer to stay with the older adult so the caregiver can have a much-needed break. Listen to the caregiver and the person receiving care to understand their concerns. Educate yourself and others on the signs of elder abuse. Most important, if you suspect abuse, notify the police and/or your local Department of Social Services.

If you are a caregiver, and feel overwhelmed or otherwise unable to carry out your caregiving commitment, first seek assistance from other friends, relatives, faith-based community, or respite care agencies. Then, find an adult day care program to relieve you of the 24/7 demands. Obtain counseling for any issues you may have that impede your ability to provide care. Substance abuse, mental health or anger problems require your immediate attention.

Emotional Abuse can be the most subtle form of injury to detect. This abuse often takes place without witnesses and can be devastating for the older person. If you notice that your loved one has withdrawn from normal activities or appears to be overly vigilant, it could be a warning sign. If the caregiver isolates the elder by preventing anyone from visiting with or speaking to the elder, a red light should go on. If you are an eyewitness to a verbally aggressive or demeaning caregiver or one who behaves in a controlling or uncaring manner, be prepared to take whatever action is necessary.

A major culprit responsible for caregiver abuse of all sorts are skilled nursing and assisted living settings, the latter of which have sprung up as lower-cost replacements for the full-care nursing facility. Despite being highly regulated by federal and state governments, 91 percent of all skilled nursing facilities lack adequate staff to properly care for patients. And worse, 36 percent of all such facilities have been in violation of elder abuse laws.

Assisted living settings are not far behind. A recent Frontline program on public television exposes the loosely regulated multibillion-dollar assisted living industry. The drive for profits often leads to fatal lapses in care. With more than one million elderly people in these facilities, many very old and in poor physical and cognitive health, deficient care and sheer neglect may be unavoidable.

The New York Times offers a highly critical view of these facilities: "pressure to keep apartments filled, labor costs low and shareholders happy increases the likelihood [of tragedies]." Wrongful death lawsuits against corporate malfeasance reveals that patients who are too sick for assisted living combined with untrained personnel and grossly under-staffed facilities contribute to a volatile care situation.

A frail loved one placed in any institutional setting requires frequent visits by family members and friends, preferably at odd times of the day and by a number of visitors over the week. Close observation over different time periods greatly reduces (but unfortunately cannot eliminate) the likelihood of abuse.

Financial Exploitation involves the unauthorized or improper use of funds, property or assets. This can involve coercing the change of a will, bank account or property transfer, taking cash or using a credit card without permission or knowledge and/or forging signatures on checks. Giving uncharacteristically excessive gifts or financial reimbursement for needed care and companionship can often go unnoticed, but suggest other common tactics used by exploiters.

Financial abuse has gained public prominence in recent years. High profile cases, such as socialite Brooke Astor, whose son looted his mother's fortune and Mickey Rooney's testimony before a Senate panel in 2011 about how he "suffered silently" for years as a family member took over his life, have brought to light how easy it is for confidants to swindle impaired persons.

Nor are misappropriated finances limited to the exceptionally wealthy and famous. A growing sense of entitlement and the ability for some people to rationalize their misconduct have contributed to an annual multi-billion dollar loss of personal wealth in the United States alone. In reality, however, only one in 14 elders who experience exploitation ever comes forward to report the abuse, according to the National Research Council.

Financial exploitation may go hand in hand with physical and emotional abuse, as well as neglect, subjecting the victim to behavior that results in fear, shame, mental anguish and emotional pain. For an older person, who has worked a lifetime to maintain and build an estate, the sense of violation may be so profound that they avoid reporting the crime to the police or even other family members.

Elder abuse thrives because it often involves relatives, trusted friends or acquaintances, and affects a largely invisible population: the dependent elderly. Similar to domestic violence and child abuse in its tragic disruption of trust and widespread suffering, elder abuse requires effective education, research, services, policy directives and advocacy at the local, state and national levels. Uncovering the prevalence and far-reaching impact of this nationwide disgrace can lead to improving the dignity, health, safety and the very basic fabric of life for all older Americans.

Afterword

Regardless of how much information we gather, caregiving continues to be a challenge. On the bright side, advances in senior health care have progressed rapidly over the last decade. Geriatric physicians are increasingly being trained to minister to the expanding number of older adults, many living into their nineties and beyond. Home care agencies, which enable sick elders to remain at home, have proliferated throughout urban and smaller cities across America. Palliative care has become a recognized standard of treatment for chronic illness and end-of-life care.

Some of the urgency for innovation and change relates to the Baby Boomer surge into retirement. An ever-growing list of housing options, both old and new, has emerged. The family home, specifically adapted for seniors, condos with elevators, shared apartments, mother-in-law units, some attached to a son or daughter's home, low-cost apartments, co-op living, retirement residences that include meals and housekeeping, and others, are all designed to allow elders to comfortably age in place.

Technology has joined forces with traditional sources of support to provide a range of equipment and services that get once immobilized elders moving again. Many city transportation systems now send smaller vans to pick up disabled persons and those who can no longer drive. More compact, easily foldable wheelchairs are available that fit into a car trunk or the back seat. Electronic monitoring systems help keep caregivers connected to isolated seniors or disabled persons. At communities across the country, medical alert systems are available to assist elders and connect them directly to a 911 operator or a trusted relative or friend. Seniors have a choice of a wristband or neck pendant type or a call button that links them directly to a monitoring system.

And, unbelievably enough, "virtual pets" can now bring comfort to residents living in care facilities. These and other futuristic inventions can enhance elder and disabled care to permit a fuller, healthier and more expansive life for millions of older Americans.

Much remains to be done, however. Caregivers often feel overworked, under-supported and under-appreciated. Given that care of the elderly and disabled is so critical to a humane social order, why do we have such a sketchy care system? Long-term care facilities cost far more than most middle class Americans can afford. In these same facilities, too few staff, often poorly trained, manage an overload of very sick and dying residents. Policymakers shun the idea of requiring better staff-to-resident ratios, because almost all facilities are now privately run and profit-oriented. Too much government interference would challenge the corporate model and be strongly resisted by managers and executives alike.

Rather than planning to spend one's last years in institutional care, America's elderly should be encouraged to age in place in their own homes. The greatest obstacle for most families is not resistance to their loved one remaining at home. Instead, it is finding affordable, well-trained home health care aides. Kaiser Health News says that pay-wise, home care workers have been treated like teenage babysitters, expected to live on near-poverty wages. Until very recently, their legal status was comparable to "companionship," although organized labor insists they're doing much more: dressing, feeding, and other medically related tasks.

New federal rules now require that home care agencies and other third party employers pay the minimum wage and overtime for full-time work. But agencies are dodging this requirement by keeping employees well under 40 hours a week. This means the disabled or elderly person will have multiple aides, instead of two to three. Kaiser Health News adds that patients "won't have the continuity of care, and particularly for people with cognitive deficits, change doesn't come easily." When the bottom line is profit, humane care tends to take a back seat.

Another tactic that promotes in-home care is to empower federal Area Agencies on Aging to offer a variety of resources for unpaid family caregivers, including information and referral, educational materials, respite care, adult day services and caregiver training, especially for Alzheimer's disease and dementia. The federal government acknowledges that 75 percent of all elder care is being provided by family and friends. A local federal office expresses it this way: "Families have always been, and continue to be, the primary source of help to those with long-term care needs."

Hospice care, among our most helpful institutions for serving the dying and their families, remains underutilized. Families tend to procrastinate in asking their physician for a referral, because that would admit that their loved one is dying. And once they call 911 for emergency care or deliver their loved one to a hospital, far too many treatments, such as cardio-pulmonary resuscitation, tracheostomy, feeding tubes and other invasive surgeries, are administered to dying patients without the solace of comfort care.

Wilfully planning a *good death* should be on everyone's personal agenda. Yet, the topic is not merely unpopular, but practically banished from everyday discourse. The overwhelming number of people still dying in hospitals, not at home or in a supportive care center with loved ones, intensifies our fear of death and underscores our neglect of planning. Jennifer Worth writes *In the Midst of Life*—a probing study of end of life care— that death continues to be viewed as shameful, an embarrassment to the family, and a failure for the attending physician. The author says:

> *The social taboo surrounding death is deep-seated, and it is most unhealthy. How has it developed? How has it sneaked up on us? The Victorians and Edwardians used to wallow in their death scenes and funerals. Why has the pendulum swung so far the other way, so that a death is neither seen nor mentioned?*

So, where do we go from here in caring for our elderly loved ones? I will once again hammer home the importance of three concerns—*awareness*, *education* and *enlightenment*—not only for caregivers, but for all of us. *Awareness:* how finite our life is, and the necessity of planning and shaping it to allow time and space for caring for others. *Education*: how much to learn about chronic illness and the end of life, and ways to create the most benign environment for caregiver and loved one. *Enlightenment*: how to recognize the remarkable benefits of providing aid and spiritual sustenance to a loved one. Yet, despite our concerted efforts to be aware, educated and enlightened, sometimes the best approach is to practice acceptance, and allow the experience to unfold.

Recommended Reading & Resources

AARP Bulletin, "Obstacles to Pain Relief." August 2010.

AARP Bulletin, "Dealing with Pain: How to Help Your Loved One." August 2010.

Carol Abaya, "Grandchildren Can Help Immensely in Elder Care." Newjerseynewsroom.com, July 13, 2012.

Daniel Abeloos, "A Troubling Trend: Senior Scams Become More Complicated and Common." http://www.losaltosonline.com/news/sections/news/202-big-picture/45170-J46742, retrieved July 29, 2013.

Susan Adcox, "Children as Caregivers for Grandparents." http://www.grandparents.about.com/grandparentingtoday/a/Children-As-Caregivers-For-Grandparents.htm/, retrieved August 17, 2013.

Administration on Aging, "Long-Term Care Ombudsman Program." www.aoa.gov/AoA_programs/Elder_Rights/Ombudsman/index.aspx, September 19, 2012.

Agingcare.com, "What is Sundowner's Syndrome?" http://www.brookdaleliving.com/sundowners-syndrome.aspx, retrieved November 13, 2013.

Agingcare.com, "The Simple Way to Keep a Senior Driver Safer Behind the Wheel." http://www.agingcare.com/News/keep-elderly-driver-safe-156964.htm, retrieved June 20, 2013.

Alzheimer's Society, "Sex and Dementia." http://www.alzheimers.org.uk.

American Legion, "Healing the Physical Injuries of War." http://www.legion.org/veteransbenefits/bulletins/90099/healing-physical-injuries-war, retrieved June 29, 2013.

American Psychological Association, "Young Caregivers." http://www.apa.org/pi/about/publications/caregivers/practice-settings/intervention/young-caregivers.aspx, retrieved August 17, 2013.

Aplaceformom.com, "Sundowners Syndrome." http://www.aplaceformom.com/senior-care-resources/articles/ sundowners-syndrome, retrieved November 30, 2013.

Shelly Barnes, "Why Seniors May Be Healthier in Assisted Living." *The Tennessean,* April 10, 2013.

Belvoir Media Group, *Healthy Years, UCLA Healthy Years.* 800 Connecticut Avenue, Norwalk, CT 06854-1631.

Amanda Bennett, *The Cost of Hope*: *A Memoir.* New York: Random House, 2012.

Pam Belluck, "In Turnabout, Children Take Caregiver Role." *The New York Times*, February 22, 2009.

Nina Bernstein, "Council Bill Would Crack Down on Proliferation of Adult Day Care Centers." *The New York Times*, June 6, 2013.

John Bingham, "Toll of Loneliness: Isolation Increases Risk of Death, Study Finds." *Telegraph.* 26 March, 2013.

Jane E. Brody, "Shaking Off Loneliness." *The New York Times.* May 13, 2013.

Jane E. Brody, "Reaching for Zen with Each Stroke and Lap." *The New York Times.* May 14, 2012.

Linda Burhans, "The 'AAA' Dilemma of Caregivers." http:// seniorholisticliving.com/the-aaa-dilemma-of-caregivers, retrieved March 30, 2013.

Caregiver Support Blog, "Being a Young Caregiver." http://www.caregiversupport.wordpress.com/2008/10/13/ being-a-young-caregiver/, retrieved August 17, 2013.

"Caring for the Caregiver." National Military Family Association. June 20, 2013.

Centers for Disease Control and Prevention, "Older Adults: Tips for Caregivers." http://www.cdc.gov/healthliteracy/ developmaterials/audiences/olderadults/tipsforcaregivers.html, retrieved August 28, 2013.

Grant Charles, Tim Stainton and Sheila Marshall, "Young Carers in Canada: The Hidden Costs and Benefits of Young

Caregiving." Ottawa, Ontario: The Vanier Institute of the Family, July 3, 2012.

Pauline Chen, "Do You Know What Your Doctor is Talking About?" *The New York Times*, April 2, 2009.

Tom Cohen, "Mickey Rooney Tells Senate Panel He was a Victim of Elder Abuse." CNN.com, March 2, 2011.

Anita Creamer, "Long-Distance Caregiving of Aging Relatives is High-Anxiety for McGeorge Law Student." *The Sacramento Bee*, August 10, 2012.

Nanette J. Davis, *Caregiving Our Loved Ones: Stories and Strategies That Will Change Your Life.* Bellingham, Washington: House of Harmony Press, 2012.

Nanette J. Davis, "Financial Security: Older Women, Cumulative Disadvantages and Retirement Consequences." *Journal of Education Finance*, Summer 2005.

James Dao, "Study Seeks Biomarkers for Invisible War Scars." *The New York Times*, February 6, 2013.

Thomas Day, "About Assisted Living." National Care Planning Council, April 19, 2013, http://www.longtermcarelink.net/eldercare/assisted_living.htm.

Division of Aging and Adult Services, "Issue Brief: Vulnerable Adult and Elder Abuse Awareness," http://www.ncdhhs.gov/aging/eaday, retrieved June 29, 2103.

Nicole Higgins DeSmet, "Advice on Addiction in Boomers." *The New York Times*, August 14, 2013.

Kathleen Doheny, "Medical Marijuana Has Merit, Research Shows." Pain Management Health Center, WebMD Health News. http://www.webmd.com/pain-management/news/20100218/medical-marijuana-has-merit-research-shows, retrieved February 5, 2013.

eCaring offers a comprehensive online-based system. http://www.ecaring.com

Richard A. Friedman, "A Rising Tide of Substance Abuse." *The New York Times*, April 29, 2013.

Lynn Feinberg and Rita Choula. "Understanding the Impact of Family Caregiving on Work, Fact Sheet 271." AARP Public Policy Institute, October 2012.

Atul Gawande, "Letting Go: What Should Medicine Do When it Can't Save Your Life?" *The New Yorker*, August 2, 2010.

Genworth Life Insurance Company of New York, The Genworth 2013 Cost of Care Survey, 10th Edition. Richmond, Virginia, 2013.

Jennifer Gerhold, "Working and Caring for Elders at the Same Time." http://www.dementiatoday/work-and-eldercare/, May 6, 2013.

Jennifer Gerhold, "What is Mild Cognitive Impairment (MCI)?" http://www.dementiatoday.com/what-is-mild-cognitive-impairment-mci/, February 20, 2013.

Jennifer Gerhold, "Celebrating the Holidays with Alzheimer's," http://www.dementiatoday.com/celebrating-the-holidays-with-alzheimers/, November 21, 2012.

Judith Graham, "Assisted Living vs. Hospice: Who's in Charge?" *The New York Times*, November 16, 2012.

Bryan Gruley, "Boomer Sex with Dementia Foreshadowed in Nursing Home." *Bloomberg News.* http://www.bloomberg.com/news/print/2013-07-22/boomer-sex-with-dementia-foreshadowed-in-nursing-home.html, retrieved July 22, 2013.

Lee Gutkind, Editor, "At the End of Life: True Stories About How We Die." Underland Press, 2012.

Melanie Haiken, "Pay for Assisted Living: 8 Smart Ways to Pay for Assisted Living." http://www.caring.com/articles/pay-for-assisted-living?print=true, retrieved April 12, 2013

Melanie Haiken, "20 Secret Signs of Addiction." http://www.healthyliving.msn.com/diseases/caregiving/20-secret-signs-of-addiction-1, retrieved October 8, 2013.

Harvard Health Letter, "Getting Out in Front of Mild Cognitive Impairment." Vol. 39, No. 1, November 2013.

Harvard Women's Health Watch, Harvard Medical School, Volume 20, Number 8, April 2013.

Harvard Women's Health Watch, "Needling Away Chronic Pain: Research Finds That Acupuncture Is an Effective Pain Reliever." Volume 20, Number 7, March 2013.

Harvard Women's Health Watch. "When Patients Suddenly Become Confused." Volume 18, Number 9, May 2011.

Highgate Senior Living, "Highgate Happenings." Bellingham, Washington, May 2013.

Charles W. Hoge & Associates, "Mild Traumatic Brain Injury in U.S. Soldiers Returning From Iraq." *New England Journal of Medicine,* Vol. 358, No. 5: January 31, 2008.

Iraq and Afganistan Veterans of America, "Traumatic Brain Injury (TBI)." http://iava.org, retrieved June 13, 2013.

Phil Izzo, "Number of the Week: More Veterans Survive, but with More Injuries." *The Wall Street Journal.* May 25, 2013.

Susan Jaffe, "Home Health Workers to Get Minimum Wage, Overtime Pay." http://blog.aarp.org/2013/09/18/home-health-workers-to-get-minimum-wage-overtime-pay/, retrieved December 20, 2013.

Erica Jacques, "When Seniors Have Chronic Pain: Diagnosing, Treating and Managing Chronic Pain in Older Adults." About.com Guide, June 3, 2010.

Peter Jaret, "Fighting Pain." *AARP Bulletin/Real Possibilities*, April 2013.

Abigail Jones, "Information Overload: How to Sort through the Slush to Find the Cancer Information You Need Online." *Coping with Cancer*, May/June 2010.

Lori Johnston, "Facing Hallucinations, Delusions and Paranoia in a Positive Way." Agingcare.com, June 19, 2012.

Marilyn Joyce, "Are You On Information Overload? Most Cancer Patients and Caregivers Are!" http://www.kickcancerinthecan.com/blog/are-you-on-information-overload-most-cancer-patients-and-caregivers-are, retrieved August 28, 2013.

Marina Kamenev, "Sex After Dementia." *The Atlantic.* http://www.theatlantic.com/health/archive/2013/06/sex-after-dementia/276489, retrieved July 22, 2013.

Bill Keller, "Heroic Measures." *The New York Times*, January 13, 2014.

Joe Klein, "Can Service Save Us?" *Time*, July 1, 2013, pp. 24–34.

Joe Klein, "The Long Goodbye." *Time*, June 11, 2012, pp. 18–25.

Nicholas D. Kristof, "When War Comes Home." *The New York Times*, November 9, 2012.

Dana Larsen, "4 Ways to Soothe Sundowner's Symptoms." http://www.aplaceformom.com/blog/2013-8-2-sundowners-syndrome/, retrieved October 8, 2013.

Kimberly Leonard, "Nursing Homes Begin to Offer Shelter for Elder Abuse Victims." *U.S. News & World Report*, March 18, 2013.

Danny Ludeman, "Fighting Elder Care Abuse." http://www.onwallstreet.com, July 29, 2013.

Stacy Lu, "Examined Lives: A Young Caregiver Helps Three Generations." TEDMED Blog, February 5, 2013.

Luis Martinez and Amy Bingham, "U.S. Veterans: By the Numbers." abcnews.co.com, November 11, 2011.

Mayo Clinic, "Sundowning: Late-day Confusion." http://www.mayoclinic.com/health/sundowning/HQ01463, retrieved November 13, 2013.

Mayo Clinic, "Early-onset Alzheimer's: When symptoms begin before age 65." http://www.mayoclinic.com/health/alzheimers/AZ00009, retrieved October 8, 2013.

Suzanne Mintz, "Caregivers Need a Break, Some 'Me Time.'" *PN Magazine*, June 2012.

David W. Myers, "A 'Sale/Leaseback' Deal Helps Parents and Kids." *The Bellingham Herald*, October 20, 2013.

The New York Times, "Marijuana: The Wonder Drug." March 1, 2007.

National Center on Elder Abuse (NCEA), "Protect Yourself from Abuse, Neglect and Exploitation," http://www.aoa.gov/YEAP. htm, retrieved June 29, 2013.

National Center on Elder Abuse (NCEA), "Warning Signs of Elder Abuse." http://www.aoa.gov/YEAP.html, retrieved June 29, 2013.

National Center on Elder Abuse (NCEA), "10 Things Anyone Can Do to Protect Seniors," http://www.aoa.gov/YEAP.htm, retrieved June 29, 2013.

NYC Elder Abuse Center, "Recent News Reports of Elder Abuse Overlook Epidemic." http://www.nyceac.com/elder-justic-dispatch-recent-news-reports-of-elder-abuse-overlook-epidemic/, retrieved on June 29, 2013.

National Public Radio, "Can Elderly Patients With Dementia Consent To Sex?" http://www.npr.org/templates/story/story. php?storyld=204580868, retrieved July 22, 2013.

Danielle Ofri, "The Challenge of Diabetes for Doctor and Patient." *The New York Times*. October 17, 2013.

Kevin B. O'Reilly, "Many Paid Caregivers Lack Health Literacy Skills." www.amednews.com, May 4, 2011.

Jim Pellegrine, "A Holiday Boost for Family Caregivers." http:// eldercare-blog.typepad.com/jim-pellegrine-blog/2012/11/a-holiday-boost-for-family-caregivers.html, November 19, 2012.

Ben Quinn, "Thousands of Children as Young as Five Act as Family Carers, Figures Show." *The Guardian*, May 16, 2013.

Karen Rainski, "A Better Way to Manage Pain." AARP Bulletin, June 1, 2011.

Kim Remesch, "Caregiving: When Your Elderly Loved One is Ill." Yahoo Voices, October 13, 2010.

Susan C. Reinhard, Carol Levine and Sarah Samis, *Home Alone: Family Caregivers Providing Complex Chronic Care.* Washington, D.C.: AARP Public Policy Institute, 2012 (http://www.aarp. org/ppi).

Rescue Alert of California, "Signs Your Aging Parent Needs a Medical Alert Device." http://www.rescuealertofca.com, August 13, 2012.

Ned Resnikoff, "Disabled Veterans Struggle With Broken Claims System." http://www.msnbc.com, May 26, 2013.

Arthur Roeser, "Caregiving, Without Answers." http://www.thecaregiverspace.org/blog/caregiver-stories/, retrieved October 16, 2013.

Barbara Ross and Corky Siemaszko, "Brooke Astor's Octogenarian Son Anthony Marshall to Get 1 to 3 Years in Prison for Looting his Mom's Fortune." *New York Daily News*, March 26, 2013.

Candace Rotolo, "Benefits at Work for Caregivers." http://www.agingcare.com/Articles/employee-benefits-for-working-caregivers-149872.htm, May 6, 2013.

Joanna Saisan, M.S.W. & Associates, "Assisted Living Facilities." http://www.helpguide.org, April, 2013.

Susan Salach, "Caregiving and Substance Abuse: Crisis Intervention." *The Working Caregiver*, January 13, 2011.

Frank Samson, "Handling the Stress of Long-Distance Caregiving." *Sonoma Valley Sun*, August 2, 2012.

May Sarton, *The House By The Sea: A Journal.* New York: W.W. Norton & Company, 1977.

Douglas Scharre, "Managing Sundowner's Syndrome." http://www.parentgiving.com/elder-care/manage-sundowner-syndrome/, retrieved October 8, 2013.

Science Daily, "Increased Rates of Hospitalization Linked to Elder Abuse." http://www.sciencedaily.com/releases/2013/04/130408172019.htm, retrieved June 29, 2013.

Science Daily, "Brain Imaging Insight into Cannabis as a Pain Killer." http://www.sciencedaily.com/releases/2012/12/121220195744.htm, retrieved February 5, 2013.

Science Daily, "How Marijuana Impairs Memory." http://www.sciencedaily.com/releases/2012/03/12030114342.htm, retrieved February 5, 2013.

Science Daily, "Medical Cannabis Provides Dramatic Relief for Sufferers of Chronic Ailments, Israeli Study Finds." http://www.sciencedaily.com/releases/2013/01/130124123453.htm, retrieved February 5, 2013.

Paula Spencer Scott, "Happy Holiday Tips for Alzheimer's Caregivers." Caring.com, November 24, 2009.

Carol Cline Schultz, *Crossing the Void: My Aphasic Journey.* Bellingham, Washington: Chuckanut Enterprises, LLC, 2010.

Pepper Schwartz, "Sex and Dementia: What Are Our Rights When We're Not Ourselves Any More?" AARP Blog Archive. Sex and Dementia Patients: Is it OK or Should It Be Stopped? July 26, 2013. http://www.blog.aarp.org/2013/07/26/pepper-schwartz-sex-and-dementia/, retrieved August 6, 2013.

"Seniors Living with Chronic Pain," Comfortkeepers.com. http://www.comfortkeepers.com/information-center/news-and-highlights/LivingWithChronicPain%20%20.

Senior Care, "What is an Ombudsman?" http://www.seniorcare.net/what-is-an-ombudsman/, February 17, 2012.

Daniel Sewell, "Elder Abuse Leads to Rise in Seniors Seeking Care at Shelters," *Huffington Post*, January 27, 2013.

Signs, symptoms and diagnosis of dementia may be found at http://www.alz.org/what-is-dementia.asp.

Smithsonian Magazine, "Marijuana Isn't a Pain Killer—It's a Pain Distracter." December 2012. http://blogs.smithsonianmag.com/science/2012/marijuana-isnt-a-pain-killer-it's-a-pain-distracter/, retrieved February 5, 2013.

Marlo Sollitto, "How to Handle an Elderly Parent's Bad Behavior." Agingcare.com, http://www.agingcare.com/Articles/bad-behavior-by-elderly-parents-138673.htm, retrieved October 8, 2013.

Paula Span, "A Dark View of Assisted Living." *The New York Times*, July 30, 2013.

Paula Span, "When Work Makes You Choose." *The New York Times*, September 14, 2012.

Statistic Brain, "Elderly Abuse Statistics." http://www.statisticbrain.com/elderly-abuse-statistics/, retrieved June 29, 2013.

Carrie Steckl, "Six Easy Steps to a Self-Care Plan for the Holidays." http://www.chicagonow.com/ask-dr-chill/2012/11six-easy-steps-to-a-self-care-plan-for-the-holidays/, retrieved December 1, 2012.

"Support for Lung Cancer Patients and Caregivers." http://www.patientpower.info/programs/support-for-lung-cancer-patients-and-caregivers, retrieved August 28, 2013.

Kimberly A. Steinhagen and Michael B. Friedman, "Substance Abuse and Misuse in Older Adults." *Aging Well*, Volume 1, Number 3, Summer 2008.

Dan Tobin, "Eight Steps for Family Caregiving, Part 2." *Psychology Today*, August 26, 2009.

T. Tanielian, R. Ramchand, M. P. Fisher, C. S. Sims, R. Harris and M. C. Harrell, "Military Caregivers: Cornerstones of Support for our Nation's Wounded, Ill and Injured Veterans." *Rand Corporation Report*, 2013.

UCLA Division of Geriatrics, "Study Finds That Loneliness Triggers Unhealthy Immune Response." *Healthy Years*. Volume 11 G-R. May 2013.

Unfrazzle, "The Challenge of Helping Young Caregivers." http://www.unfrazzledcare.com/the-challenge-of-helping-young-caregivers/, retrieved August 21, 2013.

United States Department of Veterans' Affairs, "Services for Family Caregivers of Post-9/11 Veterans." http://www.caregiver.va.gov/support_benefits.asp, retrieved November 7, 2012.

USA Today, "Study: Huge Burden on Caregivers of Military Wounded." March 8, 2013.

VNSNY Center for Home Care Policy & Research, "Chronic Pain Management." April 2009, Series C, Report 6.

WebMD, "Sundowning: Causes, Symptoms, and Treatment."
http://www.webmd.com/alzheimers/guide/sundowning-causes-symptoms-and-treatments, retrieved November 13, 2013.

WebMD, "Advanced Prostate Cancer and Caregiving."
http://www.webmd.com/prostate-cancer/guide/prostate-cancer-caregivers/, retrieved August 28, 2013.

Melody Wilding, "Veterans Day 2012: The State of America's
Aging Warriors." Ecaring.com Blog, November 7, 2012.

Mark Wiley, "Without Proper Sleep, Your Brain Fills with Toxic
Waste." http://easyhealthoptions.com/alternative-medicine/without-proper-sleep-your-brain-fills-with-toxic-waste/,
retrieved November 13, 2013.

Jacque Wilson, "CNN Heroes: Young Caregivers Put Life on
Hold." CNN.com, October 3, 2012.

David Wood, "Iraq, Afghanistan War Veterans Struggle with
Combat Trauma." *Huffington Post,* July 4, 2012.

Jennifer Worth, *In the Midst of Life*. London: Phoenix Paperback,
2011.

Lisa Duque Zilinski. "Information Behaviors of Cancer Patients in
the Information Age." *Library Student Journal*, March 2010.

About the Author

Nanette J. Davis is the author of "The ABCs of Caregiving: Words to Inspire You," "Caregiving Our Loved Ones: Stories and Strategies That Will Change Your Life," "Blessed is She... Elder Care: Women's Stories of Choice, Challenge and Commitment," eight other academic books and more than 100 professional publications. She received her Ph.D. in Sociology from Michigan State University, and completed a post-doctorate degree at Stanford University. Nanette brings more than three decades experience as an educator, writer, advocate, researcher and lecturer, and was granted the prestigious Fulbright Senior Scholar Award, among other accolades. She most recently taught at Western Washington University, Chapman University and Portland State University.